QUICK AND EASY
AIR FRYER

ABI THOMPSON
OF AIR FRYER GIRL UK

HQ

HQ
An imprint of HarperCollins*Publishers* Ltd
1 London Bridge Street
London SE1 9GF

www.harpercollins.co.uk

HarperCollins*Publishers*
Macken House
39/40 Mayor Street Upper
Dublin 1
D01 C9W8
Ireland

10 9 8 7 6 5 4 3 2 1

First published in Great Britain by
HQ, an imprint of HarperCollins*Publishers* Ltd 2026

Copyright © Abi Thompson 2026

Abi Thompson asserts the moral right to be identified as the author of this work.
A catalogue record for this book is available from the British Library.

ISBN 9780008810986

Publishing Director: Louise McKeever
Assistant Editor: Lian Wilson
Copy-editor: Rachel Pierce
Photographer: Andrew Burton
Layout Designer: Claire Rochford
Food Stylist: Pippa Leon
Prop Stylist: Faye Wears
Senior Production Controller: Halema Begum

All rights reserved. No part of this publication may be reproduced, stored in a retrieval system, or transmitted, in any form or by any means, electronic, mechanical, photocopying, recording or otherwise, without the prior permission of the publishers.

Without limiting the exclusive rights of any author, contributor or the publisher of this publication, any unauthorised use of this publication to train generative artificial intelligence (AI) technologies is expressly prohibited. HarperCollins also exercise their rights under Article 4(3) of the Digital Single Market Directive 2019/790 and expressly reserve this publication from the text and data mining exception.

Printed and bound by GPS in Bosnia and Herzegovina

Contents

- 5   Hello and Welcome
- 6   Must-have Air Fryer Accessories
- 7   Cooking Guides
- 9   Common Air Fryer Mistakes
- 10   Pantry Items
- 11   Icon Keys

12 Breakfast & Brunch
36 Lunch & Light Bites
82 Main Meals
140 On the Side
164 Sweet Treats

- 188   Index
- 192   Acknowledgements

Hello and welcome to my air fryer cookbook!

I can't tell you how excited I am to share this with you. Every recipe in here is crafted with home cooks in mind – recipes that are easy to prepare and just as easy to cook. They're for people like me who want to eat well, enjoy proper food, and still keep things simple and affordable (with the odd treat now and then!).

Air fryers have honestly changed the way I cook. Since I bought my first one back in October 2023, I've been obsessed. The fact that you can make delicious meals in such a short amount of time has been a total win for me. No more waiting ages for the oven to heat up when I get home after a long day.

Time's precious, and when you've been out of the house for 12 hours, those extra 10 or 15 minutes really matter. You just want something quick, tasty and easy to knock up – and that's exactly what the air fryer gives you.

When I first started sharing my air fryer creations online, I had no idea how many other people were just as into it as me. The community that's grown around it has been amazing, and my passion for making simple, flavour-packed meals has only got stronger. That's how this book came to life.

All the recipes inside take 30 minutes or less to cook (plus a bit of prep) and use ingredients you can find in any UK supermarket.

I hope you enjoy cooking your way through it, and that, like me, you'll soon find yourself using the oven less and less.

If you enjoy the recipes in this book and want more fresh ideas, tips and air fryer inspiration, come and find me on TikTok and Instagram @airfryergirluk! I share new recipes every week along with handy tips to make cooking even easier.

Long live the air fryer!

Abi x

aka Air Fryer Girl UK

Must-Have Air Fryer Accessories

The right accessories can take your air fryer game to the next level, making cooking easier, cleaner, and even more versatile. From perfect poached eggs to avoiding burnt fingertips, these must-have accessories will help you get the most out of your air fryer.

I've also included a few general kitchen essentials. Some might seem obvious, but they're super handy to have if you don't already own them.

AIR FRYER SPECIFIC
It's all about the silicone when it comes to air fryer cooking! I've listed my most-used accessories first, so let's dive in.

Silicone Muffin Moulds
These are brilliant for poached eggs, mini cakes, puddings, or anything with a wet base.

Silicone Tongs and Utensils
Using silicone utensils instead of metal ones helps avoid scraping or damaging the air fryer's non-stick coating. I'd recommend having at least one pair of silicone tongs and a silicone mixing spoon.

Hot Dish Tongs
Lifting things out of the air fryer can be tricky. These clever tongs hook under even the smallest of lips, helping you lift hot dishes, tins, or racks safely without the risk of burns or spills.

Silicone Mitts
Just like the hot dish tongs, these prevent you from burning your fingertips. Sometimes tongs aren't the right tool, so it's worth having both options on hand.

Paper Liners
Paper liners come in all shapes and sizes, so you should be able to find some to fit your specific model. I've found that small independent cookware shops are great places to pick them up.

With sides I use these every week for things like granola. They're ideal when you don't want ingredients falling through the holes of your crisper tray or when you just want to cut down on mess. They're thin enough for heat to pass through but still save on cleaning time.

Sheets with holes These are great when you just want to stop things sticking to the crisper tray, like pastry or fish, and the holes allow the heat to circulate evenly.

Silicone Cake Tins (10 cm/ 4 inch)
A larger version of the muffin moulds mentioned earlier, these are perfect for baking cakes in your air fryer. They're flexible, non-stick, and just the right size for a lovely Victoria sponge.

Mini Pudding Moulds (Steel)
Ideal for Yorkshire puddings, lava cakes, or individual desserts. They give a perfect result without sticking. I prefer these over silicone for Yorkshire puddings as they're sturdier and hold the hot oil better.

Racks with Skewers
These help you to maximize space in your air fryer and are great for kebabs. They're also handy for holding lighter ingredients (like nachos) in place so they don't blow around while cooking.

Cooking Guides

The more you use your air fryer, the more confident you'll become at trusting your instincts with cooking times. The timings overleaf will help you get started, but think of them as a guide rather than a rulebook. Don't be afraid to experiment!

Higher temperatures will give you a crispier finish, and you can always turn the heat up for the last couple of minutes to brown things off a bit more. I tend to do this with foods like sausages and chicken thighs for a lovely crispy skin.

Just make sure your food is cooked all the way through before tucking in. A meat thermometer is brilliant for this.

CONVERSION CHARTS

If you're converting cooking temperatures and times from food packaging or a recipe that uses a conventional oven, the charts on the next page will help you adjust them for your air fryer.

Use them as a starting point, then tweak slightly depending on your air fryer model and how crisp you like your food. All air fryers vary a little, so check on your food the first time you cook it and then adjust the time or temperature next time, if needed.

Silicone Baskets
A lot of people use these every time they cook, but for me they're the least-used accessory. They're great if you're not keen on cleaning your air fryer after each use, since you can just pop them in the dishwasher or wash by hand.

KITCHEN ESSENTIALS
These are the bits and pieces I reach for all the time when cooking. They're not specific to air frying, but they'll make life in the kitchen that bit easier.

Digital Scales
An absolute staple. I use mine constantly and would say it's the most-used item after my air fryer.

Meat Thermometer
A complete game-changer – no more overcooked chicken! It takes the guesswork out of knowing whether meat is cooked properly, and for under a tenner it's worth every penny.

Mixing Bowls
Always handy to have a range of sizes. I prefer stainless steel as they're easy to clean and last for years.

Pastry Brush
You'll want that golden pastry finish, so a good pastry brush is a must. Go for silicone so it stays air fryer-friendly.

Mini Chopper
You could manage without one, but honestly, it saves loads of time. Perfect for chopping nuts, blending herbs, or whipping up a quick pesto.

Temperatures

Oven	Fan Oven	Air Fryer
190°C	170°C	150°C
200°C	180°C	160°C
210°C	190°C	170°C
220°C	200°C	180°C
230°C	210°C	190°C

Time

Oven	Air Fryer
10 mins	8 mins
15 mins	12 mins
20 mins	16 mins
25 mins	20 mins
30 mins	24 mins
35 mins	28 mins

Oven	Air Fryer
40 mins	32 mins
45 mins	36 mins
50 mins	40 mins
55 mins	44 mins
60 mins	48 mins

COOKING TIMES FOR FRESH FOODS

These timings are here to give you a head start when you're working out how long things take to cook in your air fryer. Every air fryer is a bit different, so think of these as a guide rather than an exact rule. Learn what works for your model and your taste, and tweak as you go.

I've given a two-minute window for each food type to allow for variation between models. All timings are for fresh foods only, no frozen in sight! Most frozen foods already come with cooking instructions on the packaging, which you can easily adapt using the conversion charts. Some even include air fryer instructions now, which is definitely a step in the right direction. Truth be told, I'm not the biggest fan of frozen food, unless it's veg. Frozen veg is often fresher than 'fresh' supermarket veg since it's frozen soon after picking, so feel free to use it wherever it suits.

Veg

Food Type	Cook Time & Temp.
Jacket/Baked Potato	45–50 mins at 180°C
Homemade Chips	25–27 mins at 190°C
Sweet Potato (whole)	35–40 mins at 180°C
Sweet Potato (wedges)	25–27 mins at 190°C
Broccoli Florets	6–8 mins at 190°C
Asparagus (whole)	6–8 mins at 200°C
Cherry Tomatoes (halved)	6–8 mins at 180°C
Peppers (halved)	23–25 mins at 180°C
Mushrooms (1 cm / ½ inch slices)	13–15 mins at 180°C
Courgettes (1 cm / ½ inch slices)	13–15 mins at 190°C
Butternut Squash (2 cm / ¾ inch cubes)	20–22 mins at 190°C
Carrots (2 cm / ¾ inch cubes)	18–20 mins at 200°C
Corn on the Cob (whole)	12–14 mins at 190°C

Fish

Food Type	Cook Time & Temp.
Salmon Fillet	10–12 mins at 190°C
Prawns	6–8 mins at 180°C
Cod Fillet	10–12 mins at 200°C
Tuna Steak	10–12 mins at 180°C
Fish Cakes	14–16 mins at 180°C

Meat

Food Type	Cook Time & Temp.
Sausages	14–16 mins at 190°C
Chipolatas	10–12 mins at 190°C
Bacon	8–10 mins at 190°C
Burgers	12–14 mins at 190°C
Chicken Breasts	17–19 mins at 190°C
Chicken Thighs	26–28 mins at 190°C
Chicken Drumsticks	22–24 mins at 200°C
Pork Chops	10–12 mins at 180°C
Lamb Chops	8–10 mins at 190°C

Common Air Fryer Mistakes and How to Avoid Them!

Why use an air fryer?
Not only do air fryers generally not need to be preheated (unless your model specifies in the manual that it should), they also cook foods more quickly and save money on electricity. That's a win–win in my opinion.

Do I really need to read the manual?
Honestly … yes. Every air fryer is a bit different, and giving the manual a quick skim will help you understand how yours works. Whether it has different zones, trays or heating elements, knowing what you're working with makes a huge difference.

Why is my food coming out soggy?
It's probably because you're overcrowding the drawer. Air fryers work by circulating hot air around your food. If you cram too much in, the air can't move and things won't crisp up. Try cooking in batches or using a rack to spread food out more evenly.

Do I need to shake the drawer or flip things?
Yes – and it's one of the easiest ways to improve your results. Food near the fan cooks more quickly, so shaking halfway helps it cook more evenly. For longer cook times (like 25 minutes), I'll often shake or flip things twice.

Is it bad to keep opening the air fryer?
If you open it constantly, yes – you'll lose heat each time. A quick check is fine, but otherwise just trust the process and let the air fryer do its thing.

Do I really need to clean it every time?
Yes! A dirty air fryer can cause smoking, smells and bad results. I soak the drawer in warm soapy water while I'm eating, then wash it straight away. Most are non-stick or dishwasher safe so it's quick and easy.

Isn't the whole point that air fryers are oil-free?
Not quite. Air fryers are low oil, not no oil. A small amount of oil helps food crisp up, adds colour and improves flavour. I often use spray oil for ease.

What kind of oil should I use?
Stick to oils with a high smoke point – like rapeseed, sunflower or avocado oil (see page 10). Olive oil tends to burn in an air fryer. You can also find air fryer-safe spray oils in most supermarkets.

Can I just use oven recipes in my air fryer?
You can, but you'll need to tweak the time and temp. I usually reduce the oven temperature by 20°C and the cooking time by 20 per cent. I've included several handy conversion charts opposite so if in doubt, check those out.

Do I need special accessories?
Not necessarily, but they'll make your life easier! Anything oven-safe can usually go in an air fryer – ramekins, small roasting dishes, silicone moulds, baking parchment. They're brilliant for keeping mess to a minimum and expanding what you can cook. You can check out my recommended accessories on page 6.

What's the difference between Air Fry and Max Crisp?
Not all air fryers have this setting, but if yours does, Max Crisp cooks at a higher temperature and is great for frozen or breaded foods like chips or nuggets, or for adding extra crunch at the end of cooking. I often use it just for the last few minutes to crisp things up. For most recipes, though, stick with the regular Air Fry mode for more control and even cooking.

Pantry Items

There are a few ingredients I always keep on hand for those last-minute dinners or to save an extra trip to the shop. You don't need to buy everything at once, but having a few of these stocked up makes cooking so much easier. My spice drawer looks like I could open a shop, but there are definitely some key things I use time and time again!

THE RIGHT OIL – essential for air fryer cooking

- You'll want a high-smoke-point oil, ideally in a spray bottle. Avocado and rapeseed are great choices, or grab an air fryer-friendly spray from the supermarket. Low-smoke-point oils can leave food tasting bitter or burnt.
- Truffle oil – totally unnecessary, but good for the taste buds. A drizzle takes any meal up a notch.

ALWAYS HANDY TO HAVE IN …

The Fridge
These items have a good shelf-life and are perfect for knocking up a last-minute dinner when you've got nothing else in.

- Chorizo – adds instant flavour to anything from eggs to pasta.
- Pancetta – great for crisping up and adding a salty bite to salads or bakes.
- Feta – crumbles beautifully over roasted veg or grains.
- Cream cheese – a handy base for sauces or quick dips.
- Parmesan – makes everything better, enough said.
- Spring onions – perfect for finishing off dishes or adding freshness to savoury recipes.
- Garlic – keeps away vampires (and makes everything taste better).

The Freezer
I'm not a massive fan of freezer food, but these are the things that are absolutely worth keeping stocked up. They've saved me more times than I can count.

- Puff pastry – a freezer hero. Sweet or savoury, it saves the day every time.
- Frozen veg (peas in particular!) – the easiest way to sneak in one of your five-a-day.
- Brioche bread, rolls, bagels and wraps – always handy when you forget to get bread. Defrost overnight or give them a quick zap in the microwave.

HERBS AND SPICES

There are a few basic herbs and spices that I reach for constantly. They add instant flavour to just about everything.

- Garlic granules
- Chilli flakes
- Smoked paprika
- Oregano
- Parsley
- Cinnamon
- Cumin
- Black pepper
- Salt

SAUCES AND CONDIMENTS

My holy grail of condiments. They elevate the flavour of any meal.

- Soy sauce
- Sweet chilli sauce
- Balsamic glaze
- Pesto (red or green)
- Miso paste
- Harissa paste
- Honey
- Maple syrup

- Marmite
- Mayonnaise
- Ketchup
- American or Dijon mustard

TINS AND JARS
- Butter beans – breakfast, lunch or dinner, they're so versatile.
- Roasted red peppers – a quick way to add sweetness and colour to a dish.
- Capers or gherkins – salty little bursts of flavour that lift sauces, salads and fish dishes.

DRY GOODS
- Pasta, macaroni and microwaveable rice – always handy for a quick side dish.
- Gnocchi – the centrepiece for a super-quick and easy dinner.
- Panko or breadcrumbs – because everything tastes better breaded.

BAKING
A few bits that are always worth having in for when the baking mood strikes.

- Plain flour
- Self-raising flour
- Rolled oats
- Mixed nuts
- Mixed seeds
- Raisins
- Caster sugar
- Light brown sugar
- Golden syrup
- Bicarbonate of soda
- Baking powder
- Cocoa powder
- Vanilla extract

Build your pantry over time – start with the basics, then add flavour-boosters and special extras as you go.

KEY

Vegan

Vegetarian

Meat

Seafood

30-minute timer

Breakfast & Brunch

Fluffy French Toast with Bacon & Blueberries

 PREP TIME 10 MINUTES

 COOK TIME 10 MINUTES

 SERVES 1

This is one of my favourite weekend breakfasts, for when I actually have time to stop. Soft, custardy brioche with crisp edges, smoky bacon and juicy blueberries – it's simple, but feels like a treat. I love the saltiness of the bacon paired with the sweetness of the dish. Finish with a drizzle of maple syrup and a dusting of icing sugar for that extra touch. I love this dish, I hope you do too!

120 ml / 4 fl oz milk or cream
2 large eggs
½ tsp ground cinnamon
1 tsp vanilla extract
3 slices brioche bread
3 rashers streaky bacon
Icing sugar, for dusting
Maple syrup, for drizzling
1 handful blueberries

1. In a large bowl, whisk together the milk/cream, eggs, cinnamon and vanilla extract.

2. Pour your mixture into a shallow dish and add your slices of brioche bread in a single layer to soak up the mixture. Flip the slices over after a couple of minutes so all sides are covered.

3. Add a liner to your air fryer drawer and transfer your bread into the drawer. Pour over any remaining mixture on top of the bread slices.

4. If you have space to do so, lay your streaky bacon strips in a single layer alongside your bread and cook together. If you don't have space, cook your bacon separately so it's ready at the same time.

5. Air fry for 10 minutes at 180°C.

6. Plate up your bread, followed by a dusting of icing sugar (best to use a sieve for this if you have one), a drizzle of maple syrup, your blueberries and bacon.

TIP

Veggie option: If you're not a bacon fan, this works beautifully with Greek yoghurt instead.

Easy Egg Taco Boats

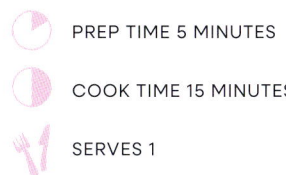

PREP TIME 5 MINUTES

COOK TIME 15 MINUTES

SERVES 1

These look like you've gone to loads of effort – but they take no time at all. Soft tortilla boats filled with savoury egg, crispy bacon and a bit of veg to balance it out. Great for a weekend brunch or a 'bit more than toast' kind of breakfast. I always recommend adding the cheese because it just makes it! But if you're watching calories you can always leave it off.

BREAKFAST AND BRUNCH

1 egg
1 tbsp milk
1 tbsp grated Parmesan
1 soft tortilla boat
1 spring onion, sliced
1 rasher cooked streaky bacon
3 asparagus spears
1 handful grated Cheddar cheese (optional but highly recommended!)
Black pepper, freshly cracked

1. Whisk together the egg, milk, Parmesan and a crack of black pepper in a jug.

2. Place the tortilla boat into your air fryer drawer.

3. Add the sliced spring onions and crispy bacon to the boat, then pour over the egg mixture.

4. Top with the asparagus spears and sprinkle over the Cheddar (if using).

5. Air fry at 180°C for 15 minutes until golden and puffed up.

6. Let them cool slightly before tucking in.

TIP

These work really well with different fillings– try swapping the bacon for smoked salmon or chopped mushrooms, or using spinach instead of asparagus. You can also batch-cook a few at once if your air fryer has space.

Egg, Marmite & Cheesy Crumpets

PREP TIME 5 MINUTES

COOK TIME 8 MINUTES

SERVES 1

My sister introduced me to the Marmite-and-egg combo on holiday once, and I've loved it ever since! It works so well with the crumpets and cheese in this dish – salty, gooey, savoury and properly satisfying. It takes a tiny bit more effort than your usual toast-and-egg situation, but it's so worth it. A solid option for when you need a Marmite fix and don't mind a little more work!

2 crumpets
1 handful grated Cheddar cheese
1 tsp unsalted butter
1 tsp Marmite
2 medium eggs

1. Cut out the centre of the crumpets, being careful not to cut all the way through (as your egg will ooze out if you do!). Dice up the middle of the crumpet that you've removed and add to a bowl with the Cheddar cheese, then stir to combine.

2. Butter inside the hollowed-out parts of the crumpets, then do the same with the Marmite.

3. Place a liner in your air fryer drawer, place the crumpets on top and crack an egg into the hollow in each crumpet. (I crack into a bowl first and pour in from the bowl, avoiding any issues with the egg shell!) Sprinkle the crumpet and cheese mixture on top of each crumpet and place in the air fryer for 8–10 minutes at 180°C for a runny egg, or longer if you prefer a firmer egg. (Each air fryer is different, so you may find you need to increase the cooking time depending on your model.)

TIP

Not into Marmite? Try replacing it with pesto instead.

Creamy Garlic Mushrooms & Crispy Pancetta on Sourdough

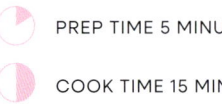

PREP TIME 5 MINUTES

COOK TIME 15 MINUTES

SERVES 1

Golden mushrooms, crispy pancetta and creamy garlic cheese all piled onto toasted sourdough – proper comfort food, but still packed with flavour. The air fryer gives the mushrooms a lovely texture and the garlic-and-herb soft cheese melts into everything like a dream. It's quick to make and works any time of day – brunch, lunch or even a light dinner.

125 g / 4½ oz chestnut mushrooms, sliced into 1 cm / ½ inch pieces
Oil spray
40 g / 1½ oz diced smoked pancetta pieces
1 tsp garlic-and-herb soft cheese
1 large or 2 small slice(s) sourdough bread
Salt and pepper

1. Pop the sliced mushrooms into your air fryer drawer, spray with oil and season with salt and pepper.

2. Air fry at 180°C for 15 minutes, shaking every 5 minutes.

3. When 7 minutes remain, add the pancetta pieces to the drawer and continue cooking.

4. Once done, tip the mushrooms and pancetta into a bowl and stir through the garlic-and-herb soft cheese until creamy and coated.

5. Toast your sourdough in the air fryer for 5 minutes at 180°C, flipping halfway if needed.

6. Spoon the creamy mixture onto the toast and serve straight away.

TIP

Veggie option: Leave out the pancetta. If you want to make it more filling, top with a poached egg or serve with wilted spinach, or a simple side salad. If you want it even creamier, add a drop of single cream when mixing through the cheese.
For non-veggies, you can swap the pancetta for chopped bacon.

Smoky Shakshuka with Butter Beans

 PREP TIME 5 MINUTES

 COOK TIME 14–16 MINUTES

 SERVES 1

This is a really lovely brunch dish when you want something warm and filling that's still a bit different. It's vegetarian, but the butter beans give it that satisfying, almost meaty texture. The spices bring depth and warmth, and the soft egg finishes it off perfectly. I love scooping it straight out of the dish and piling it onto toast.

BREAKFAST AND BRUNCH

1 tbsp oil
1 tsp smoked paprika
½ small garlic clove, finely grated, or ¼ tsp garlic purée
½ tsp ground cumin
½ tin chopped tomatoes
½ tin butter beans, drained and rinsed (keep juice to one side)
3 tbsp juice from the beans
1 spring onion, finely sliced
½ roasted red pepper from a jar, roughly chopped
½ tsp dried parsley
1 medium egg
Salt and pepper

TO SERVE
Fresh parsley
Crusty bread/sourdough

1. Place the oil, paprika, garlic and cumin into an air fryer-friendly dish and air fry at 190°C for 2 minutes to warm through and release the flavour.

2. Meanwhile, mix the chopped tomatoes, butter beans and juice, spring onion, red pepper and dried parsley in a jug. Season with a pinch of salt and plenty of black pepper.

3. Once the 2 minutes are up, carefully tip the tomato mixture into the warm dish and stir to combine with the oil and spices. Air fry for 15 minutes at 190°C, stirring halfway through. (Ensure the mixture is bubbling away before the next stage so that the egg white cooks through properly. If it isn't, add a couple more minutes to the cooking time.)

4. After the 15 minutes are up, gently crack the egg into the centre and air fry for another 7 minutes at 180°C, until the egg white is just set and the yolk is still soft. (I like to crack it into a small dish first to avoid any eggshell slipping in!)

5. Finish with chopped fresh parsley and an extra crack of black pepper. Serve with toasted sourdough: 5 minutes in the air fryer at 180°C, flipping halfway.

Want to make it even fancier? Crumbling some feta on top works beautifully with the smoky flavours and adds a salty tang.

Feta, Beans & Egg Bowl

 PREP TIME 5 MINUTES

 COOK TIME 12 MINUTES

 SERVES 1

A cosy little brunch bowl that takes barely any effort but feels like you've made something proper. The beans go smoky with the bacon, the feta adds a bit of tang, and that soft egg on top is just asking to be dipped into with buttery sourdough soldiers. Quick, hearty and exactly what I want when I've held out for a mid-morning brunch.

½ tin baked beans
1 handful crispy bacon bits
1 handful chopped spring onion
1 medium egg
1 handful crumbled feta
Black pepper

TO SERVE
Toasted sourdough soldiers

1 In an air fryer-friendly dish or ramekin, add the baked beans, crispy bacon bits and chopped spring onion. Give it a quick stir to mix everything together.

2 Make a well in the centre and crack in your egg. Season with freshly cracked black pepper and sprinkle crumbled feta on top.

3 Air fry at 180°C for 12 minutes, until the egg is just set and the top is golden.

4 Carefully remove the dish (it'll be hot!) and serve straight away with toasted sourdough soldiers for dipping.

Add whatever you've got to hand – chopped cherry tomatoes, a few baby spinach leaves or even some leftover roast veg. Grated Cheddar or crumbled goat's cheese also works well as an alternative to the feta.

Quick & Easy Egg Cups

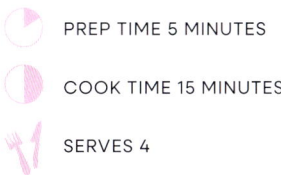

PREP TIME 5 MINUTES

COOK TIME 15 MINUTES

SERVES 4

½ bag baby spinach
4 medium eggs
½ red onion, diced
1 handful grated mature Cheddar cheese
Salt and pepper

These are great served warm or stored in an airtight container for a snack the following day. I love making a batch of these at the start of the week – they're super easy to make, protein-packed and a nice alternative to your regular breakfast options.

1. Add the baby spinach to a colander over a saucepan, pour over boiling water and leave to wilt for 5 minutes. Once the 5 minutes have passed, use the back of a spoon to squeeze out as much water as possible from the spinach, then set to one side.

2. Crack each of the eggs into their own muffin/cake mould. (I use a four-section silicone mould, but you can use individual moulds if that's all you have.) Season with salt and pepper. Add a sprinkle of the diced red onion, cooked spinach and Cheddar cheese into each mould and stir. Top with a little more cheese.

3. Transfer the egg cups to the air fryer drawer and air fry for 15 minutes at 190°C.

BREAKFAST AND BRUNCH

TIP

Try mixing up the fillings depending on what you've got in the fridge – leftover roasted veg, bits of ham, crumbled feta … whatever works!

Breakfast Brioche with Mushrooms, Chorizo & Poached Eggs

- PREP TIME 5 MINUTES
- COOK TIME 12 MINUTES
- SERVES 2

This is one of my absolute faves in the book – it's got that sweet-savoury combo I love! It is inspired by a veggie breakfast I used to order at Bill's, a cosy restaurant chain mainly in the South of England – they served mushrooms with hummus and it was chef's kiss. The meaty mushrooms and spicy chorizo work so well together, especially when finished with a drizzle of sweet chilli. Sounds a bit rogue, but trust me – it's banging!

125 g / 4½ oz flat mushrooms, sliced into 1 cm / ½ inch strips
Oil spray
2 medium eggs
60 g / 2 oz chorizo, diced
2 brioche burger buns, sliced
2 heaped tsp hummus
Salt and pepper

TO SERVE
Sweet chilli sauce

1. Add the mushrooms to your air fryer drawer, spray with a little oil, and season with salt and pepper. Air fry at 190°C for 12 minutes.

2. Meanwhile, spray two small silicone moulds with oil and add about 1 cm / ½ inch of boiling water to each. Crack the eggs into ramekins first, then gently pour into the moulds.

3. With 7 minutes remaining, add the egg moulds into your second drawer. If using a single drawer, keep the mushrooms to one side and place the moulds in beside them, being careful not to spill.

4. With 5 minutes left, give the mushrooms a stir and add in the diced chorizo. Stir again gently to coat everything in the lovely juices.

5. Pop your sliced brioche buns into the air fryer for the last 2 minutes to toast.

6. Spread 1 heaped teaspoon of the hummus onto each toasted bun base. Top with the mushroom and chorizo mix.

7. Carefully pour the water from the egg moulds and gently lift out the eggs with a spoon. Place one egg on top of each bun base.

8. Drizzle generously with sweet chilli sauce, place each bun lid on top and dig in!

TIP

This works best with a dual-drawer air fryer, which allows you to cook the eggs and fillings at the same time. But it's still totally doable in a single drawer – just stir the mushrooms and chorizo carefully with a spatula rather than shaking.

Easy Eggs

Eggs can be one of the trickiest things to master in an air fryer because every model cooks slightly differently – but once you've cracked it (pun intended!), you'll never look back.

Soft- and Hard-Boiled Eggs

 PREP TIME 1 MINUTE

 COOK TIME 9–12 MINUTES

SERVES – FLEXIBLE, AS MANY AS YOU'D LIKE

Fresh eggs (straight from the fridge)

1. Place the eggs directly into the air fryer drawer.

2. Air fry at 150°C for 9 minutes for soft-boiled (runny centre, great for dipping); 12 minutes for hard-boiled (set yolk, ideal for slicing).

3. Once cooked, immediately transfer the eggs to a bowl of ice-cold water and leave for a couple of minutes to stop the cooking process.

4. Peel and serve, or slice the top off for the perfect dippy-egg moment.

Poached Eggs

 PREP TIME 3 MINUTES

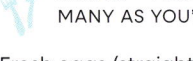 COOK TIME 9–10 MINUTES

SERVES – FLEXIBLE, AS MANY AS YOU'D LIKE

Fresh eggs (straight from the fridge)
Oil spray

1. Lightly spray some silicone moulds with oil.

2. Add around 1 cm / ½ inch of boiling water to each mould – just enough to cover the tops of the eggs.

3. Crack your eggs into ramekins first (this helps avoid any shell), then gently pour them into some silicone moulds.

4. Transfer the moulds to your air fryer drawer and cook at 190°C for 8 minutes for a soft yolk. If you like them firmer, cook for 9–10 minutes.

5. Carefully tip out any excess water before serving – I find using a spoon to lift out each egg works best.

TIP

I always use eggs straight from the fridge and base my timings on medium eggs – if yours are at room temperature, shave off a minute to get the same results.

Mixed Berry Compote

PREP TIME 5 MINUTES

COOK TIME 18 MINUTES

SERVES 5

Juicy, jammy and bursting with flavour – this berry compote is a total winner. I love how easy it is to make using frozen berries, so you can get that summery hit any time of year! Just throw it all in a dish, let the air fryer do its thing, and you've got the perfect topping for granola, pancakes, yoghurt or ice cream. Yum!

BREAKFAST AND BRUNCH

300 g / 10½ oz frozen mixed berries
1 tbsp caster sugar (adjust to taste)
Zest of 1 lemon
Juice from ½ lemon
1 tsp vanilla extract (optional)

1. Add the frozen berries to an air fryer-friendly dish – one with high sides works best to catch all those gorgeous juices. Sprinkle over the sugar, lemon zest and juice, and the vanilla extract (if using). Give it a quick stir.

2. Air fry at 180°C for 18 minutes, giving it a stir a couple of times throughout. The berries will soften and release their juices – the longer you cook it, the more syrupy it gets.

3. Stir again once it's done, then leave to cool slightly.

4. Serve warm over your favourite sweet treat, or let it cool fully before transferring to a sealed container and popping it in the fridge.

TIP

This is dreamy with thick Greek yoghurt and a handful of my Super-nutty Cinnamon Granola (see page 30). I keep a batch in the fridge in an airtight container for up to a week and dip in for a big spoonful each morning.

Super-nutty Cinnamon Granola

 PREP TIME 5 MINUTES

 COOK TIME 20 MINUTES

 SERVES 5

This is one of my most-cooked air fryer recipes – I make a batch every single week. It started out as a Joe Wicks recipe I found on the Body Coach app (when I was on a bit of a health kick), but I've tweaked it over time into this nutty, cinnamon-packed version that I genuinely crave. I love that it uses apple sauce as a natural sweetener – something I always have in the cupboard – and that it's packed with nuts, seeds and spice. I usually serve it with Greek yoghurt and berries for a quick, satisfying breakfast.

100 g / 3½ oz rolled oats
120 g / 4 oz mixed nuts, roughly chopped
60 g / 2 oz mixed seeds
1 tsp cinnamon
40 g / 1½ oz coconut oil, melted
70 g / 2½ oz apple sauce
40 g / 1½ oz honey
80 g / 2¾ oz raisins
Salt

TO SERVE
Mixed Berry Compote (see page 29)
Greek yoghurt

1. Combine the rolled oats, mixed nuts, seeds and cinnamon in a large bowl.

2. In a separate bowl/jug, stir together the melted coconut oil (I melt mine in a jug in the microwave for 2 minutes), apple sauce, honey and a pinch of salt and pour into the bowl with the dry ingredients. Mix together until fully combined.

3. Add a paper liner to your air fryer drawer and transfer the mixture in an even layer onto the liner.

4. Air fry for 20 minutes at 150°C, stirring every 5 minutes. When 3 minutes remain, mix in the raisins.

5. Once finished, allow the granola to cool, then break up with a wooden spoon. Serve in a bowl with Greek yoghurt and Mixed Berry Compote. The granola will keep well in an airtight container for up to one week.

TIP

Keep any empty glass jars (like the one from your apple sauce) and reuse them to store your granola in handy portions – ideal for grab-and-go breakfasts!

Harissa Poached Eggs with Spinach & Peppers

 PREP TIME 10 MINUTES

 COOK TIME 8–10 MINUTES

 SERVES 1

Soft poached eggs, spicy harissa-roasted peppers and juicy tomatoes, piled on top of wilted spinach and a toasted muffin – this is a quick but impressive breakfast or brunch dish that feels like a treat!

BREAKFAST AND BRUNCH

50 g / 1¾ oz baby spinach
80 g / 2¾ oz cherry tomatoes, halved
60 g / 2 oz roasted red peppers from a jar, sliced
2 tsp harissa paste
½ tsp dried oregano
Oil spray
1–2 medium eggs
Black pepper

TO SERVE
1 muffin, sliced

1 Place the spinach in a colander over a saucepan. Pour over boiling water and leave for 5 minutes to wilt, then press with the back of a spoon to squeeze out as much water as possible.

2 Add the tomatoes and peppers to an air fryer-friendly dish. Stir through the harissa and oregano, spray lightly with oil, and season with black pepper.

3 Depending on how hungry you are, use one or two eggs. Lightly spray a small silicone dish for each egg with oil. Add about 1 cm / ½ inch boiling water to each – just enough to cover the tops of the eggs. Crack the eggs into a ramekin first, then gently pour into the silicone dishes.

4 Place both the harissa-tomato-pepper dish and the eggs into the air fryer. Air fry at 190°C for 9 minutes, stirring the tomatoes halfway through. For softer egg yolks, cook for 8 minutes; for firmer yolks, cook for 10 minutes.

5 While everything cooks, toast your muffin. To serve, top the muffin base with the wilted spinach, then the harissa-tomato-pepper mixture. Gently lift the poached eggs from the silicone dishes (carefully tipping away the water first) and place on top.

6 Finish with a final crack of black pepper and enjoy straight away.

TIP

Crack the eggs into a ramekin before pouring into the silicone moulds – this makes it easier to avoid any shell pieces and gives you a neater finish.

Spinach, Sun-dried Tomato & Goat's Cheese Frittata

 PREP TIME 5 MINUTES

 COOK TIME 25 MINUTES

 SERVES 2

This one's so easy to throw together, and it tastes even better the next day. It's ideal for lunches or light dinners when you want something quick but still feels like you've made an effort. The creamy goat's cheese and soft spinach work perfectly with the fluffy eggs, and the air fryer gives it a lovely golden top.

75 g baby spinach
5 medium eggs
4 tbsp milk
3 spring onions, sliced
4 sun-dried tomatoes, finely chopped
½ block (around 60 g / 2 oz) soft goat's cheese, crumbled
Salt and pepper

1. Start by wilting your spinach – to do this, pop the spinach in a colander, over a saucepan, and pour boiling water over it. Leave to wilt for 5 minutes, then drain out as much of the water as possible by pushing down the spinach with the back of a spoon.

2. Crack the eggs into a large bowl and whisk together with the milk, then add the spring onions and season with salt and pepper.

3. Place a silicone dish into your air fryer drawer, and if you have a paper liner, place it in the dish (it makes it easier to lift the frittata out).

4. Pour the mixture into the lined dish, break up the spinach evenly, scatter the sun-dried tomatoes evenly, then add the crumbled goat's cheese.

5. Air fry for 25 minutes at 170°C.

6. Once finished, use a fork to lift the silicone dish from the air fryer (place it through both handles).

7. Allow to cool for 5 minutes, pull the paper liner from the silicone dish, cut up and enjoy!

TIP

Add a handful of cooked, chopped potatoes to bulk it out. You can also swap goat's cheese for feta or Cheddar.

Lunch & Light Bites

The Best Ever Burrata Salad

 PREP TIME 5 MINUTES

 COOK TIME 8 MINUTES

 SERVES 1 AS A MAIN (OR 2 AS A STARTER)

I absolutely LOVE burrata, and this salad is one of my favourites – sweet, salty, creamy and crunchy all at once. The warmth of the nectarines brings out therir natural sweetness, while the Parma ham crisps up beautifully in the air fryer. Paired with creamy burrata and a drizzle of balsamic glaze and some crunchy croutons, it's simple, satisfying and full of flavour.

2 nectarines, stoned and quartered
Oil spray
3 slices Parma ham
1 ball burrata

FOR THE CROUTONS
Leftover crusts or white bread
Oil spray
Garlic granules
Dried parsley

TO SERVE
Mixed salad leaves
Balsamic glaze
Black pepper

1. First, prepare the croutons. Dice the bread into 1 cm / ½ inch cubes. Add to a bowl and spray with oil, a light sprinkle of garlic granules, and a pinch of dried parsley. Toss to coat. (This crouton recipe is given in full on page 45.)

2. Place the nectarines in a single layer in the air fryer drawer and spray lightly with oil. Nestle the Parma ham beside them – it crisps up fast, so keep it flat and spread out.

3. If using a dual-drawer air fryer, pop the croutons in the second drawer at the same time. If using a single drawer, add the croutons in with the nectarines and Parma ham – just make sure there's space for everything to be in a single layer.

4. Air fry everything at 180°C for 8 minutes, turning the nectarines halfway through and giving the croutons a shake or stir. Keep an eye on the Parma ham – it should crisp up in 3–5 minutes, so remove it early if needed. The croutons should be golden and crisp by the end of the 8 minutes, but if they need a little extra time, pop them back in for 1–2 minutes until perfectly crunchy.

5. To serve, scatter salad leaves on a plate, top with the nectarines, tear over the Parma ham and break up the burrata in the centre.

6. Finish with a handful of garlic croutons, a drizzle of balsamic glaze and a crack of black pepper.

TIP

This works beautifully with all sorts of soft fruits. Try swapping the nectarines for peaches, plums or even figs depending on the season. Each one brings a slightly different flavour, but they all pair brilliantly with the creamy burrata and salty Parma ham.

The Ultimate Tuna Bagel Melt

 PREP TIME 10 MINUTES

 COOK TIME 6 MINUTES

 SERVES 1

LUNCH AND LIGHT BITES

I've been making these for years in the oven, but the air fryer makes them even quicker to knock up! Hot, cheesy and packed with flavour – it's the kind of lunch that feels comforting but takes hardly any time. The tuna mix is loaded with salty, savoury extras, and the golden top is always the best bit.

1 tin tuna, drained
2 spring onions, thinly sliced
2 sun-dried tomatoes, finely chopped
2 gherkin slices, finely chopped or 1 tsp capers, chopped
½ tsp Dijon mustard
2 tbsp mayonnaise
1 bagel
1 handful grated mature Cheddar cheese
Black pepper

1. In a small bowl, combine the tuna, spring onions, sun-dried tomatoes, gherkins or capers, mustard, mayonnaise and a good crack of black pepper.

2. Slice your bagel in half and spoon on the tuna mixture to both sides, patting down with a fork to keep it in place.

3. If you have a paper liner, add one to your air fryer drawer (this just saves a bit of the mess but it's not a big deal if you don't have any). Then add your tuna-topped bagel.

4. Sprinkle the grated cheese over the bagel halves and pat down with the back of your hand to prevent the cheese flying about in the air fryer.

5. Air fry for 6 minutes at 190°C, then serve.

TIP

Try adding a pinch of chilli flakes for a little heat. If you're out of bagels, this works just as well on crumpets (controversial, I know!) or muffins.

Scotch Eggs

 PREP TIME 10 MINUTES

 COOK TIME 21 MINUTES

 SERVES 2

These always remind me of summer picnics when I was younger – Scotch eggs are such a classic, and homemade ones are next level. I use ready-made sausages for ease (I always seem to have some in the fridge!), but you can use sausage meat if you prefer. They make a proper tasty snack and are way easier to make than you might think.

3 medium eggs (2 whole for the centre, 1 beaten for coating)
3 sausages (good-quality ones!) or 200 g / 7 oz sausage meat
3 tbsp plain flour
1 tsp smoked paprika
6 tbsp panko breadcrumbs
Oil spray
Salt and pepper

TO SERVE
English mustard or some pickle (optional)

1. Place two of the eggs in the air fryer drawer and air fry for 9 minutes at 180°C. Once finished, use tongs to transfer the eggs from the air fryer into a bowl of iced water to cool down, then peel. (This can be a bit fiddly but persevere, it's worth it!)

2. Meanwhile, remove the skin from the sausages and combine into one ball, then split the mixture into two portions. Pat the sausage mixture down until you have an even layer of meat (about 1.5 cm / ½ inch thick).

3. Place one peeled egg in the middle of the sausage mixture and wrap the sausage around it. Roll it in your hands until it's an even thickness all around the egg and completely sealed. Repeat for the second egg.

4. You'll need three medium-sized bowls for the next bit … add the plain flour and smoked paprika to one bowl and season with salt and pepper, add the beaten egg to another, and put the breadcrumbs in the final bowl.

5. Roll a sausage ball into the flour, then dip in the beaten egg until fully coated and finish with the breadcrumbs, ensuring an even layer all the way round. Repeat for the second sausage ball.

6. Place the sausage balls into the air fryer and spray with oil. Air fry for 12 minutes at 200°C. This should give you a perfectly cooked, crispy outer layer and a lovely soft egg! Serve with a dollop of English mustard or some pickle if you like.

TIP

Supermarkets offer loads of flavoured sausages, so mix it up and try out various flavours, depending on what mood you're in!

7-minute Pesto Pitta Pizzas

 PREP TIME 5 MINUTES

 COOK TIME 7 MINUTES

 SERVES 2

These make such a quick and tasty lunch – all the pizza flavour, none of the waiting around. I've used red pesto, mozzarella and pepperoni here, but feel free to switch up the toppings with whatever you've got in the fridge. Great for when you want something warm and satisfying in under 10 minutes.

4 tsp red pesto
2 pitta breads
Dried oregano
6 slices of pepperoni
1 ball mozzarella, shredded
2 tbsp grated mature Cheddar
Fresh basil (optional but highly recommended!)

1. Spread the pesto evenly across both pitta breads, leaving about ½ cm / ¼ inch around the edge.

2. Sprinkle with dried oregano, then top with the pepperoni, shredded mozzarella and grated Cheddar cheese. Lightly press the grated cheese down to prevent it from blowing around in the air fryer.

3. Place the pittas in the air fryer drawer and cook at 180°C for 7 minutes.

4. Once ready, transfer to a serving plate and top with fresh basil (if using).

TIP

Try mixing up the base with red pesto, green pesto, or even tomato purée with herbs. Use whatever cheese you've got and chuck on any toppings that need using up.

Garlic & Herb Croutons

 PREP TIME 5 MINUTES

 COOK TIME 4–6 MINUTES

 SERVES – FLEXIBLE, DEPENDING ON HOW MANY YOU NEED TO MAKE!

Leftover crusts or white bread
Oil spray
Garlic granules (to taste)
Dried parsley

I spotted a similar hack on the All Recipes website ages ago. I skip the butter and use spray oil – it works just as well! It's ideal for using up leftover bread or crusts so nothing goes to waste. In just a few minutes you've got crunchy, garlicky croutons – perfect for scattering over salads or soups.

1. Dice the bread into 1 cm / ½ inch cubes (or larger if you'd like chunkier croutons).

2. Add to a bowl, spray liberally with oil, then sprinkle with garlic granules and parsley. Toss until evenly coated.

3. Transfer to the air fryer drawer in a single layer. Air fry at 190°C for 4–6 minutes, shaking halfway, until golden and crispy. For chunkier croutons, add an extra 1–2 minutes.

TIP

If you fancy chunkier croutons, go for an uncut loaf and cube it into bigger pieces – just add a couple of extra minutes to the cooking time. Garlic granules are stronger than you think, so go easy – a little goes a long way!

Chicken Shawarma Pitta Pockets

 PREP TIME 10 MINUTES

 COOK TIME 19 MINUTES

 SERVES 4 FOR LUNCH, 2 FOR DINNER

FOR THE CHICKEN
400 g / 14 oz boneless, skinless chicken thighs
1 tbsp oil
Juice of ½ lemon
1 tsp ground cumin
1 tsp ground coriander
½ tsp smoked paprika
½ tsp turmeric
½ tsp cinnamon
½ tsp garlic granules
Salt and pepper

FOR THE YOGHURT DRESSING
2 tbsp Greek yoghurt
1 tbsp mayonnaise
Juice of ½ lemon
Fresh parsley and mint, finely chopped
Black pepper

TO SERVE
Pittas (2 per person)
Salad (e.g. shredded lettuce, tomato, cucumber)
Sweet chilli sauce (optional)

OK, so it's not cooked on a traditional rotating spit, but the spices give you all those same delicious flavours. This is a great one to prep ahead and air fry just before serving.

1. Slice the chicken thighs into thin strips (around 1 cm / ½ inch thick). Add to a bowl with the oil, lemon juice, and all the spices and garlic granules. Season with salt and pepper, then toss everything together until coated. Leave to marinate for at least 10 minutes (or overnight if you can).

2. Transfer the chicken to your air fryer drawer in a single layer. Air fry at 190°C for 16 minutes, shaking halfway through, until cooked through and crisped at the edges.

3. While the chicken cooks, mix together all the dressing ingredients in a bowl.

4. When the chicken is done, transfer to a bowl and warm your pittas in the air fryer for 3 minutes at 180°C, turning halfway.

5. To serve, cut open the pittas and (if using) spread with a little sweet chilli sauce (trust me, the sweet, punchy kick is so good). Fill with salad, chicken, a drizzle of the yoghurt dressing and an extra sprinkle of herbs.

LUNCH AND LIGHT BITES

TIP

Veggie option: Halloumi works well instead of the chicken. Follow the same instructions but reduce the cooking time to 10–12 minutes.

These also make a brilliant next-day lunch. If you're packing them up, let everything cool before filling the pittas to avoid sogginess, and keep the tomatoes and cucumber separate until you're ready to eat (if you can).

Creamy Garlic Butter Beans on Toast with Chorizo

 PREP TIME 5 MINUTES

 COOK TIME 29 MINUTES

 SERVES 1 AS LARGE PORTION (OR AS 2 SMALLER PORTIONS)

This is a flavour-packed dish. The beans turn soft and creamy, the chorizo adds a smoky richness, and the rosemary brings a lovely depth that makes it feel way fancier than your average beans on toast. I first saw the bean method on a Jamie Oliver programme and it's stuck with me ever since. It takes a few steps, but it's still simple and so worth the effort – great for a hearty breakfast, lunch or even a tasty dinner.

60 g / 2 oz chorizo, diced into ½ cm cubes
2 sprigs fresh rosemary
1 tin butter beans (including the liquid)
1 tsp red wine vinegar
100 g / 3½ oz cherry tomatoes
2 slices sourdough bread
Salt and pepper

1. Remove the crisper tray from your air fryer drawer. Add the diced chorizo and air fry for 6 minutes at 190°C, until it's crisped up and releasing those lovely oils.

2. Use a slotted spoon to lift the chorizo out and set aside, leaving the oil behind in the drawer.

3. Add the rosemary sprigs to the chorizo oil and air fry for 3 minutes at 190°C.

4. Once done, pour in the full tin of butter beans (liquid included), add the red wine vinegar, a pinch of salt and a generous crack of black pepper. Stir well. (If the rosemary leaves have come away from the stalks, remove the woody stalks now.)

5. Air fry at 200°C for 20 minutes, giving it a stir every 5 minutes until the beans are thick and creamy.

6. While the beans cook, add the cherry tomatoes to the second drawer (or cook first if using a single drawer). Air fry for 5–6 minutes at 190°C until soft and starting to blister. Toast your sourdough until golden and crisp.

7. To serve, place your toast on a plate, spoon over the creamy beans, and top with the crispy chorizo and juicy roasted tomatoes. Yum.

TIP

If you've got a single-drawer air fryer, cook the cherry tomatoes first and set them aside. Then crack on with the beans and chorizo – it all comes together beautifully. I find cheap tins of beans (supermarket own-brand!) work best here as the juice is usually a bit thicker. Fancy a green boost? Stir through some wilted spinach once the beans are ready.

Chicken, Pesto, Sun-dried Tomato & Parmesan Wrap

 PREP TIME 5 MINUTES

 COOK TIME 9 MINUTES

 SERVES 1

I tried this combo years ago in a local deli and I've been recreating it at home ever since. It's packed with flavour and is a solid option when I want something warm, quick and properly satisfying. It's cheesy, crispy and full of flavour – the pesto and sun-dried tomato combo never fails. Plus, it's a brilliant way to use up leftover chicken. You get that melty middle and golden toasted wrap with hardly any effort thanks to the air fryer.

90 g / 3 oz cooked chicken, finely diced
1 tbsp green pesto
1 tbsp grated Parmesan
2 sun-dried tomatoes, finely chopped
20 g / ¾ oz baby spinach, torn up
1 large tortilla wrap
Balsamic glaze (optional, but highly recommended for a sweet note)
Black pepper

TO SERVE
Rocket and tomato – for a simple salad

1. Add the cooked chicken to a bowl with the pesto, Parmesan, chopped sun-dried tomatoes, and baby spinach. Season with black pepper and mix everything together until well combined.

2. Lay your wrap flat and spoon the chicken filling into the centre. Drizzle over a little balsamic glaze (if using).

3. Fold in both sides of the wrap, then fold the bottom over and roll tightly to form a sealed parcel.

4. Place the wrap seam-side down in the air fryer basket. Air fry at 180°C for 9 minutes, until golden and crisp.

5. Slice in half and serve with a simple rocket and tomato salad.

TIP

If you're cooking the chicken from scratch, I recommend using boneless, skinless thighs. Slice into 1 cm / ½ inch strips, spray with a little oil, season with salt and pepper and air fry at 190°C for 14–16 minutes, until cooked through.

Roasted Tomato, Bacon & Basil Soup

 PREP TIME 10 MINUTES

 COOK TIME 18 MINUTES

 SERVES 2

A comforting classic with a smoky bacon twist. This is a soup that takes me back to my first ever waitressing job – I couldn't get enough of the homemade soup, but the bacon takes it to a whole new level. Roasting everything in the air fryer brings out big flavour with very little effort – perfect for a cosy lunch or light dinner.

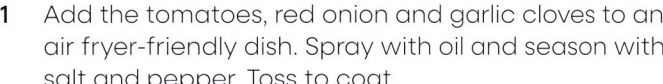

300 g / 10½ oz cherry tomatoes (or chopped tomatoes)
1 small red onion, cut into wedges
2 small garlic cloves, peeled
Oil spray
2 rashers smoked bacon
5–10 fresh basil leaves
200 ml / 7 fl oz vegetable stock
Salt and pepper

TO SERVE
Single cream (optional)

1 Add the tomatoes, red onion and garlic cloves to an air fryer-friendly dish. Spray with oil and season with salt and pepper. Toss to coat.

2 Place a rack over the veg and lay the bacon on top. (If you don't have a rack, cook the bacon first – this just needs 8 minutes at 180°C – then set aside before roasting the veg.)

3 Air fry at 180°C for 18 minutes, removing the bacon after 8 minutes if you're doing it together. Give the veg a shake, then continue roasting for the remaining 10 minutes.

4 Add the bacon and roasted veg to a blender (or transfer to a bowl if using a hand-held blender), along with the fresh basil and vegetable stock, then blend until smooth. If you're using a blender, make sure it's heatproof and suitable for hot liquids – some plastic jugs aren't!

5 Serve with a drizzle of single cream (if using).

TIP

This soup is lovely on its own but even better with a cheesy toastie or a handful of homemade croutons (just tear up some bread, spray with oil and sprinkle over garlic granules, then air fry for 5–6 minutes). Want to take it even further? Air fry a little pancetta or crispy bacon and sprinkle on top when serving.

Baked Feta with Nduja & Roasted Peppers

 PREP TIME 5 MINUTES

 COOK TIME 14 MINUTES

 SERVES 2 (AS A LIGHT MEAL OR SHARING DISH)

This fiery take on baked feta is my twist on the viral feta trend. Creamy feta is baked with nduja, cherry tomatoes and roasted red peppers until soft and bubbling, then finished with a scattering of toasted pine nuts for crunch. Served with toasted sourdough or crispbreads for scooping, it's the ultimate sharing dish.

100 g / 3½ oz cherry tomatoes, halved
100 g / 3½ oz roasted red peppers from a jar, sliced
1–2 tsp nduja paste
1 small garlic clove, finely chopped (or ½ tsp garlic purée)
½ tsp dried oregano
200 g / 7 oz block feta cheese
Oil spray
1 tbsp pine nuts (or walnuts)
Black pepper

TO SERVE
2–4 slices sourdough (or sourdough crispbreads)

1. Place the tomatoes and peppers in an air fryer-friendly dish. Mix through the nduja paste, garlic and oregano, then place the block of feta on top. Spray with a little oil and finish with extra oregano and a crack of black pepper.

2. Air fry at 180°C for 14 minutes, until the feta is soft and golden, the tomatoes are bursting and the nduja has melted into the juices.

3. Meanwhile, toast the pine nuts (or walnuts) in a dry pan over a medium heat for 2–3 minutes until golden and fragrant.

4. Remove the dish from the air fryer, scatter with the toasted pine nuts, and serve immediately with toasted sourdough or crispbreads for scooping.

Use roasted peppers from a jar in oil – they're full of smoky flavour and save on prep time. For a finishing touch, just before serving drizzle with honey or hot honey for sweetness or extra heat. This works brilliantly with harissa too, and pairs with anything crispy, from toasted sourdough to sourdough crispbreads.

Salmon Fish Finger Wraps with Lemon Mayo Slaw

 PREP TIME 10 MINUTES

 COOK TIME 10 MINUTES

 SERVES 2

Crispy golden salmon fish fingers, a creamy lemon slaw and soft tortilla wraps – this is my fresh twist on classic fish finger wraps. The lemony slaw cuts through the richness of the salmon and ties everything together perfectly.

1. Slice each salmon fillet into strips about 1 cm / ½ inch thick (you'll usually get 2–3 strips per fillet).

2. You need three bowls: to one bowl, add the plain flour, garlic granules, paprika, oregano, salt and pepper and mix until combined. Crack and beat the egg in the second bowl. Add the breadcrumbs to the third bowl.

3. Coat each salmon strip in the flour mixture, then dip in the egg, and finally press into the breadcrumbs until evenly coated.

4. Place the salmon fingers in the air fryer drawer, spray lightly with oil, and cook at 190°C for 10 minutes, flipping halfway through and spraying again, until golden and crisp.

5. While the fish cooks, make the slaw. In a bowl, mix together the mayonnaise, lemon zest and juice, sesame seeds, parsley and a good crack of black pepper. Stir through the cabbage, carrot and spring onion until evenly coated, then set aside.

6. Warm the wraps in the air fryer for the final minute of cooking, or heat them in the microwave for 10–20 seconds.

7. To build the wraps, layer with lettuce or spinach, top with the salmon fingers, then spoon over the lemon mayo slaw. Wrap up and enjoy!

FOR THE SALMON FINGERS
2 skinless salmon fillets (approx. 120 g / 4 oz each)
40 g / 1½ oz plain flour
½ tsp garlic granules
½ tsp smoked paprika
½ tsp dried oregano
1 medium egg
4 tbsp breadcrumbs (panko, if possible)
Oil spray
Salt and pepper

FOR THE LEMON MAYO SLAW
2 tbsp mayonnaise
Zest of ½ lemon
Juice of 1 lemon
1 tsp sesame seeds
1 tbsp chopped parsley
100 g / 3½ oz shredded white or red cabbage (or a shop-bought slaw mix)
1 medium carrot, grated
1 spring onion, finely sliced (add more if you like it oniony!)
Black pepper

FOR THE WRAPS
4 large soft tortilla wraps
A handful of lettuce or baby spinach leaves

 **TIP** If you fancy an extra bit of zing, finish with a drizzle of sweet chilli sauce – I literally put this with everything!

Easy-peasy Cheese & Chive Scones

 PREP TIME 10 MINUTES

 COOK TIME 15 MINUTES

 SERVES 10–20 DEPENDING ON PASTRY-CUTTER SIZE

These are so quick and easy, and you'd never guess they only need a handful of ingredients. The chives give a lovely savoury hit, and they're insanely good warm with a thick layer of butter – or, even better, sandwiched with a slice of extra Cheddar.

300 g / 10½ oz self-raising flour
180 g / 6 oz mature Cheddar, grated
10 g / ½ oz fresh chives, finely chopped
250 g / 8½ oz Greek yoghurt

TO SERVE
Butter

1. In a large bowl, mix together the self-raising flour with 130 g / 4½ oz of the grated cheese and the chopped chives. Stir in the Greek yoghurt until a dough forms.

2. Tip the dough onto a lightly floured work surface and knead gently a few times until smooth.

3. Pat the dough down and roll out with a lightly floured rolling pin to around 2 cm / ½ inch thick. Using a round cutter, cut out as many scones as you can. Re-roll any leftover dough and cut out more until it's all used.

4. Transfer the scones to the air fryer drawer, sprinkle with the remaining cheese and cook at 170°C for 15 minutes, until golden and puffed.

5. Allow to cool slightly, slice in half, spread generously with butter and tuck in!

LUNCH AND LIGHT BITES

TIP

Try switching the chives for chopped spring onion, or adding a pinch of smoked paprika for a flavour twist. You can also freeze any leftovers and reheat them in the air fryer for a few minutes to bring them back to life.

Crunchy Marmite Butter Beans

 PREP TIME 5 MINUTES

 COOK TIME 15 MINUTES

 SERVES 2–4 IN SNACK SIZED PORTIONS

If you're a fan of Twiglets, you're going to love these. That deep, savoury Marmite flavour clings to the crispy little beans like a hug for your tastebuds. They're salty, crunchy, and seriously moreish – perfect for a quick snack, a pre-dinner nibble, or even as a savoury topper for salads and soups.

LUNCH AND LIGHT BITES

1 tin butter beans, drained and rinsed
Oil spray
1 tsp Marmite or yeast extract

1. Drain and rinse the butter beans, then tip into the air fryer drawer, spray liberally with oil and air fry for 10 minutes at 180°C.

2. When the 10 minutes are up, tip the butter beans into a bowl and stir in the Marmite or yeast extract. (This might sound like a bit of extra faff – to remove the beans and then put them back in – but the beans and Marmite won't mix evenly in the drawer, so using a bowl is the best way to do this. Trust me!)

3. Transfer the coated butter beans back into the air fryer and air fry for another 5 minutes at 180°C.

4. Allow to cool for a couple of minutes, then tip into a bowl and enjoy!

TIP

These are best served straight from the air fryer but if you have leftovers (unlikely as they're so moreish!), you can keep them in an airtight container for a couple of days, crisping them back up in the air fryer for a couple of minutes when you want to tuck in again.

Brie & Chorizo Savoury S'mores

 PREP TIME 10 MINUTES

 COOK TIME 10 MINUTES

 SERVES 2 PEOPLE AS A STARTER, 6–8 AS A CANAPÉ

I can't explain how good these are! Oozy melted Brie with flavour-packed chorizo, topped with a sweet chilli jam, all squished between crunchy Ritz crackers – a taste sensation! These are a full-on flavour bomb. Great for a fancy party snack, or an indulgent starter. Ready in just 10 minutes.

1 block of Brie
12 slices of ready-sliced chorizo
24 Ritz crackers

TO SERVE
Sweet chilli jam

1. Slice the Brie into pieces around 1 cm / ½ inch thick.

2. Fold a slice of chorizo around each piece of Brie and place them tightly side by side (cheese side up) in an air fryer-friendly dish.

3. Air fry at 180°C for 10 minutes, until the cheese is melted and bubbling.

4. Carefully transfer the dish to your serving board or plate. Spoon a little sweet chilli jam over the top of the melty Brie-and-chorizo mix.

5. To serve, use a knife or spoon to lift out a piece of cheesy goodness, pop it on a Ritz cracker, and sandwich it with another cracker.

TIP

Switch up the crackers depending on what you've got– Ritz are great for that buttery crunch, but mini crostini or toasted sourdough slices work brilliantly too if you want something a bit sturdier.

Caramelized Onion & Goat's Cheese Tarts with Rocket Salad

 PREP TIME 10 MINUTES

 COOK TIME 17 MINUTES

 SERVES 6

Crispy, golden pastry topped with sweet onion chutney and creamy goat's cheese - simple ingredients that just work. These are great served warm with a balsamic-dressed rocket salad, but they're just as tasty eaten cold the next day. Ideal for lunch, a light dinner, or as part of a picnic-style spread when you want something a bit fancy with minimal effort.

320 g / 11 oz sheet ready-rolled puff pastry
180 g / 6 oz French goat's cheese
1 jar caramelized onion chutney
1 egg, beaten (for egg wash)
Cherry tomatoes
Rocket leaves
Balsamic dressing (mix together 1 part balsamic vinegar with 2 parts extra-virgin olive oil, along with a pinch of salt and pepper)

1. Cut the pastry sheet into six equal rectangles.

2. Slice the goat's cheese into 12 even rounds.

3. Add 2 heaped teaspoons of caramelized onion chutney to the centre of each pastry rectangle. Spread evenly, leaving a 1 cm / ½ inch border all the way around.

4. Place two slices of goat's cheese on top of the chutney on each tart.

5. Brush the edges of the pastry with egg wash. If you have a paper liner, pop it in your air fryer drawer – if not, don't worry; it still works well! If cooking these in batches, place the uncooked pastries into the fridge to cool until you need them.

6. Air fry at 170°C for 17 minutes, until golden and puffed up.

7. Transfer to a serving tray to allow to cool slightly.

8. While the tarts are cooling, put together your rocket salad. Halve the cherry tomatoes, add them to the rocket leaves in a bowl, then drizzle over the balsamic dressing.

TIP

You can also make mini versions using smaller squares of pastry for party food or picnics – these are always a crowd-pleaser!

Kale Crisps

 PREP TIME 5 MINUTES

 COOK TIME 4–5 MINUTES

 SERVES 2

Crispy, salty and seriously moreish, these kale crisps are a brilliant alternative to a bag of potato crisps. They're quick to make, light yet satisfying, and you can customize them with any seasoning you like, from smoky paprika to garlic salt. Perfect for when you fancy a healthier snack that still feels like a treat.

LUNCH AND LIGHT BITES

200 g / 7 oz kale
Oil spray
Salt and pepper

1. Wash and drain the kale in a colander, then tip into a large bowl.

2. Remove any woody stalks from the leaves and cut any large ones in half so they're all a similar size.

3. Spray with oil and season with salt and pepper, or your favourite spices.

4. Toss well so all the leaves are evenly coated.

5. Place the leaves in the air fryer drawer and put an air fryer rack on top to prevent them blowing around.

6. Air fry for 4–5 minutes at 180°C. Keep a close eye on them, as they crisp up quickly and can burn if left too long.

7. Once crispy, tip into a bowl and enjoy straight away.

TIP

Make sure the kale is completely dry before cooking, otherwise it can steam instead of crisping up.

Spanakopita Bites

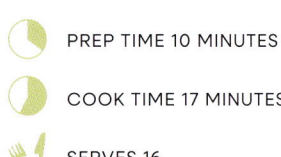

PREP TIME 10 MINUTES

COOK TIME 17 MINUTES

SERVES 16

I love these! Quick and easy to knock up for a tasty air fryer snack. The mix of salty, creamy feta, earthy spinach and flavour-packed sun-dried tomatoes is dreamy.

150 g / 5 oz baby spinach
200 g / 7 oz block feta, crumbled
10 sun-dried tomatoes, finely chopped
6 sheets filo pastry
1 medium egg, beaten (for egg wash)
Black pepper

1. Add the baby spinach to a colander over a saucepan, pour over boiling water and leave to wilt for 5 minutes, then use the back of a spoon to squeeze out as much water as possible. Chop finely.

2. Transfer the chopped spinach to a bowl with the crumbled feta and the finely chopped sun-dried tomatoes. Season with black pepper and stir until everything is combined.

3. Lay three sheets of filo pastry on top of one another on a chopping board and spoon half of the mixture along one side (lengthways) until you have an even sausage-like shape all the way along.

4. Roll the pastry tightly around the mixture and, just before the end, brush the beaten egg along the edge to seal the pastry before finishing the roll. Cut the roll into eight pieces.

5. Repeat Steps 3 and 4 for the second set of three sheets with the leftover mixture.

6. Place the rolls in the air fryer, brush with the beaten egg and air fry for 17 minutes at 170°C, turning halfway through cooking.

TIP

These are fab warm or cold, so they're great for packed lunches, picnics or parties. You can also make them ahead and reheat in the air fryer for a few minutes to bring back that lovely crispiness!

Red Pesto & Cheese Bites

 PREP TIME 10 MINUTES

 COOK TIME 18 MINUTES

 SERVES 12

Flaky, cheesy, and full of flavour – these bites are ridiculously moreish! The combo of rich red pesto and melty Cheddar wrapped in golden puff pastry makes them perfect for snacking, sharing, or serving up at a party. You only need a handful of ingredients, and the air fryer does all the hard work.

LUNCH AND LIGHT BITES

320 g / 11 oz sheet ready-rolled puff pastry
1 jar red pesto
100 g / 3½ oz mature Cheddar cheese, grated
1 medium egg, beaten (for egg wash)

1. Lay out the puff pastry sheet and cut in half widthways so you have two even sections.

2. Spread an even layer of red pesto across the first section of pastry and sprinkle with the grated cheese.

3. Place the second half of the pastry on top of the base and cut in half widthways, then cut each section in half so you have four strips.

4. Cut each strip into three so you end up with 12 sections.

5. Carefully transfer the pastry bites to your air fryer drawer and brush with egg wash for a golden bake.

6. Air fry for 18 minutes at 180°C.

TIP

I find it's easier to remove the air fryer drawer, remove the crisper plate from the drawer, place the bites on top of the crisper plate, and then carefully insert the crisper plate back into the drawer.

Devils on Horseback

 PREP TIME 5 MINUTES

 COOK TIME 8 MINUTES

 SERVES 12

4 rashers streaky bacon
12 pitted dates

One of the easiest and tastiest party snacks going. These little bites are salty, sticky and sweet all at once - moreish and always the first thing to disappear from the plate.

1. Start by cutting the streaky bacon in half lengthways, then in half widthways, so you end up with four evenly sized strips from each piece.

2. Tightly wrap each date in a piece of bacon and transfer to the air fryer drawer.

3. Air fry for 8 minutes at 180°C.

4. Transfer to a serving dish, stab each one with a cocktail stick for easy picking, serve up and enjoy!

TIP

Add a little square of cheese (like goat's cheese or blue cheese) inside the date before wrapping for an extra hit of savoury goodness – or try brushing the bacon with maple syrup for the last couple of minutes of cooking time for a sweet-salty glaze.

Cheesy Garlic Bread Bites

 PREP TIME 5 MINUTES

 COOK TIME 7 MINUTES

 SERVES 2–3

Sometimes the simplest recipes are the most irresistible, and this one is proof. My sister gave me the idea, and it's become a go-to! Using a shop-bought garlic baguette and fresh mozzarella, you can create gooey, golden bites that taste just like a restaurant treat. They're perfect for sharing.

1 ready-made garlic baguette
1 ball mozzarella

TO SERVE
Fresh basil or pesto (optional)

1. Slice or pull apart the garlic baguette into individual pieces, then spread around the garlic butter that's already on each slice.

2. Top each piece with a slice of mozzarella.

3. Line the air fryer drawer with an air fryer liner and arrange the slices in a single layer.

4. Air fry for 7 minutes at 190°C until the cheese is golden and bubbling.

5. Serve hot, finishing with fresh basil or a drizzle of pesto if you like.

TIP

Mix things up with your toppings. Fresh basil or a drizzle of pesto give a lovely herby finish, but you could also add chilli oil for heat, caramelized onions for sweetness, or even a handful of rocket on top for a fresh touch.

If you're not vegetarian, then you could add chorizo on top – it gives them a smoky kick that makes them even harder to resist.

Pigs in Blankets, Brie & Cranberry Sausage Rolls

 PREP TIME 10 MINUTES

 COOK TIME 18 MINUTES

 SERVES 10

These are next-level sausage rolls! Think pigs in blankets, melted Brie and a dollop of cranberry sauce all wrapped in golden puff pastry – they're as good as they sound. I first spotted a similar idea on TikTok and had to try it. Safe to say, they've earned a permanent spot on my party snack list!

LUNCH AND LIGHT BITES

5 rashers streaky bacon
10 cocktail sausages
1 triangle Brie
320 g / 11 oz sheet ready-rolled puff pastry
½ jar cranberry sauce
1 medium egg, beaten (for egg wash)

1. Cut the streaky bacon in half and roll a strip tightly around each sausage.

2. Cut the Brie into 10 slices, each ½ cm thick.

3. Cut the pastry sheet in half widthways, setting one section to the side.

4. Place five of the bacon-wrapped sausages along the bottom of the pastry, butting up against one another, then cut the pastry between the sausages so you end up with five strips of pastry.

5. Place a teaspoon of cranberry sauce to the side of each sausage, along with a slice of Brie.

6. Brush egg wash along the top strip of the pastry and roll each section from the sausage end up, until fully secured.

7. Repeat Steps 4–6 with the remaining ingredients.

8. Transfer the sausage rolls into the air fryer drawer and use a sharp knife to gently score the top of each one with a criss-cross.

9. Brush with a little more beaten egg and air fry for 18 minutes at 180°C.

10. Once cooked, use a spatula to transfer the sausage rolls onto a rack and leave to cool (if you can resist not tucking in straight away!).

TIP

These are delicious warm from the air fryer, but also taste great cold – perfect for buffet tables or next-day packed lunches. If you've got any leftover cranberry sauce, serve a little on the side for dunking.

Carrot & Parsnip Peel Crisps

 PREP TIME 5 MINUTES

 COOK TIME 10 MINUTES

 SERVES 2

I first saw Becky Excell making a version of these with a mix of veg peel and spices, but I've stripped it back to just carrot and parsnip, which is definitely my favourite combination. Seasoned simply with salt and pepper, they make such a good snack and are a perfect use of the air fryer. Even better, they're a brilliant way to cut down on food waste by turning peel you might normally throw away into something tasty and crunchy.

Peel from 1 bag of carrots
Peel from 1 bag of parsnips
Oil spray
Salt and pepper

1. Wash and thoroughly dry the carrot and parsnip peel, then combine with oil spray, salt and pepper in a bowl. Tip into the air fryer drawer.

2. Air fry for 10 minutes at 190°C, stirring halfway through. If they haven't crisped up as much as you'd like, pop them back in for a couple more minutes.

3. Tip into a bowl and try to stop yourself eating the whole lot!

TIP

For the best crunch, wash and dry the peel really well before cooking, otherwise it'll steam instead of crisp. Mix up the flavours with smoked paprika, garlic powder or curry powder, and don't just snack on them – they're also brilliant sprinkled over soups or salads for extra crunch.

Sweet or Savoury Pitta Chips

 PREP TIME 5 MINUTES

 COOK TIME 8 MINUTES

 SERVES – FLEXIBLE: THEY'RE EASY TO MAKE FOR 1 OR SCALE UP TO SHARE

These are such a tasty snack and super easy to knock up. I first tried a version of this when doing the Body Coach programme by Joe Wicks. (His snack ideas are next level – definitely worth checking out if you haven't already!) His version is oven-baked, but I've adapted it for the air fryer and tweaked the flavours to suit me. Just a few simple ingredients, but they really hit the spot when you fancy something crunchy – sweet or savoury.

LUNCH AND LIGHT BITES

2 pitta breads

SWEET OPTION – CINNAMON SUGAR
Oil spray
15 g / ½ oz caster sugar
½ tsp ground cinnamon

SAVOURY OPTION – GARLIC & HERB
Oil spray
1 tsp mixed herbs
¼ tsp garlic granules

1. Cut the pitta breads into 1 cm / ½ inch squares and place in a bowl. Spray with oil, then mix through either the sweet or savoury coatings. (If you have a two-drawer air fryer, why not do a batch of each at the same time?)

2. Transfer the coated pitta pieces to the air fryer drawer in an even layer and cook at 190°C for 8 minutes, shaking halfway.

3. Tip into a bowl and tuck in while warm, or leave to cool and store in an airtight container for later.

TIP

If you're counting calories, half a pitta = 1 portion in Joe's eyes ... but they're seriously moreish, so good luck! If you're making ahead, they'll keep well in an airtight container for a couple of days.

Crostini with Roasted Tomatoes & Goat's Cheese

 PREP TIME 10 MINUTES

 COOK TIME 21 MINUTES

 SERVES 4 – MAKES AROUND 20 CROSTINI

Golden, garlicky crostini topped with sweet roasted tomatoes and tangy goat's cheese. This makes such an easy but impressive snack or starter, and the flavours are spot on.

1 bake-at-home baguette roll (approx. 150 g / 5 oz – the type you get in a two-pack in supermarkets)
Oil spray
1 garlic clove
1 tsp dried parsley
250 g / 8½ oz cherry tomatoes
½ tsp dried oregano
100 g / 3½ oz soft goat's cheese (or feta), crumbled
Salt and pepper

TO SERVE
Fresh basil leaves (optional)

1. Slice the baguette into 1 cm / ½ inch-thick rounds. Spray lightly with oil, rub with the cut side of the garlic clove, and sprinkle with parsley on both sides.

2. Place the crostini slices in the air fryer at 180°C for 9 minutes, shaking every few minutes, until golden and crisp.

3. Halve the cherry tomatoes, place in an air fryer-friendly dish, spray with oil, sprinkle with oregano, and season with salt and pepper. Air fry at 190°C for 12 minutes until softened and caramelized.

4. Once cooked, transfer the roasted tomatoes to a serving dish, then scatter with the goat's cheese and top with fresh basil leaves (if using). Serve with the crunchy crostini and tuck in!

TIP

If you have a two-drawer air fryer, you can cook the bread and tomatoes at the same time. If using a single drawer, cook the bread first, then let it cool while you roast the tomatoes.

Camembert Three Ways

There's nothing quite like gooey, melted Camembert – the ultimate crowd-pleaser that feels fancy but is secretly so easy. Whether you're after something rich and savoury, sweet and sticky, or a little bit extra wrapped in puff pastry, these three versions have you covered. Pictured on page 191.

#1 Creamy Camembert with Spicy Chorizo

 PREP TIME 5 MINUTES

 COOK TIME 15 MINUTES

 SERVES 2–4

250 g / 8½ oz Camembert (whole wheel)
60 g / 2 oz chorizo

TO SERVE
Serve with Crostini (see page 78, Steps 1 and 2) or toasted baguette for the perfect dipping situation

1. Remove all packaging from the Camembert and place it in an air fryer-friendly dish. Or you can unwrap and leave it in the wooden box if it came with one – most are oven-safe and fine to go straight in the air fryer (just check the label first to be sure) – which also means less washing up!

2. Score the top diagonally both ways to make a criss-cross pattern.

3. Air fry at 180°C for 15 minutes.

4. Meanwhile, finely dice the chorizo (remove the skin first if using a chorizo ring).

5. When 5 minutes remain, open the air fryer and scatter the chorizo on top of the cheese and return to the air fryer for the final 5 minutes so the oils infuse into the cheese.

TIP

Whichever version you make, always score the top of the Camembert before cooking. It helps everything melt evenly and lets the flavour seep right in.

 PREP TIME 5 MINUTES

 COOK TIME 15 MINUTES

SERVES 2–4

250 g / 8½ oz Camembert (whole wheel)
Garlic-infused olive oil
Chilli flakes
Honey

#2 Honey & Garlic Camembert

1. Remove all packaging from the Camembert and place it in an air fryer-friendly dish (or you can unwrap and leave it in the wooden box if it came with one, as suggested opposite).

2. Score the top diagonally both ways to make a criss-cross pattern. Drizzle with the garlic-infused olive oil, sprinkle over the chilli flakes, and finish with a drizzle of honey.

3. Air fry at 170°C for 15 minutes, until golden and melted in the centre.

 PREP TIME 5 MINUTES

 COOK TIME 20 MINUTES

 SERVES 2–4

320 g / 11 oz sheet ready-rolled puff pastry
250 g / 8½ oz Camembert (whole wheel)
2 tbsp red onion chutney
1 small egg, beaten (for egg wash)

#3 Camembert & Red Onion Chutney in Puff Pastry

1. Lay out the puff pastry sheet and place the wheel of Camembert (with all packaging removed) towards one end, leaving an even border around all edges.

2. Cut the pastry into a square large enough to wrap around the cheese (save the rest for another recipe – try my Red Pesto & Cheese Bites on page 69).

3. Spoon the chutney on top of the Camembert, then fold in each corner of the pastry to form a parcel.

4. Pinch the corners together to seal, brush the parcel with egg wash and transfer to the air fryer drawer.

5. Air fry at 180°C for 20 minutes, until golden and crisp.

Main Meals

The Best Ever Coronation Chicken

 PREP TIME 10 MINUTES

 COOK TIME 20 MINUTES

 SERVES 6–8

This always goes down a storm! The chicken cooks quickly and easily in the air fryer, and the creamy, curried dressing with mango and pomegranate gives it loads of flavour. Perfect as a showstopper salad for a BBQ or party spread, or batch-prepped for lunches through the week.

1 kg / 2 lb chicken breasts
Oil spray
430 ml / 15 fl oz mayonnaise
6 tsp curry powder
1 jar mango chutney
2 celery sticks, diced
1 fresh mango, half diced into cubes and the other half sliced lengthways
1 handful of pomegranate seeds
4 Little Gem lettuces
1 handful chopped coriander
Salt and pepper

1. Place your chicken breasts in an even layer in the air fryer, spray with a little oil and season with salt and pepper. Air fry for 20 minutes at 180°C or until cooked through.

2. Leave the chicken to cool while you make the coronation sauce.

3. For the sauce, combine the mayonnaise, curry powder and mango chutney in a large bowl.

4. Shred the chicken breasts with two forks; use one fork to hold the chicken in place and the other to shred the meat.

5. Tip the chicken into the sauce, along with half of the celery, the diced mango and half of the pomegranate seeds. Mix together until everything is evenly combined.

6. Wash and dry your lettuce leaves and layer up around a large serving dish.

7. Spoon the chicken mixture into the lettuce leaves and scatter with the pomegranate seeds. Serve with the remaining celery, sliced mango and a sprinkle of coriander.

TIP

This makes an amazing jacket potato filling or sandwich filler. Just don't skip the toppings – the fresh mango and pomegranate seeds add the perfect balance.

Homemade Chicken Nuggets

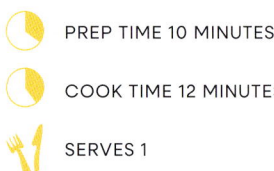

- PREP TIME 10 MINUTES
- COOK TIME 12 MINUTES
- SERVES 1

MAIN MEALS

You can't beat homemade nuggets. Crispy, golden and packed with flavour, they're miles better than anything shop-bought. A fun one to make with the kids, too – just make sure they wash their hands after handling the raw chicken!

1 chicken breast
Oil spray
1 tsp peri peri seasoning
2 tbsp plain flour
1 small egg, beaten
4 tbsp breadcrumbs
Salt and pepper

1. Cut the chicken breast into 3 cm / 1 inch chunks and add to a bowl. Spray with a little oil and mix in the peri peri seasoning.

2. You'll need three medium bowls for the next step: add the plain flour to one bowl (season with salt and pepper), the beaten egg to another, and the breadcrumbs to the final bowl.

3. Coat your chicken pieces with the flour, followed by the egg, then finish with an even layer of breadcrumbs.

4. Place the chicken nuggets in a single layer in the air fryer drawer and spray with oil.

5. Air fry for 12 minutes at 180°C, or until the chicken is cooked through, flipping halfway through and spraying with oil again.

TIP

I love these with some crispy fries and a big dollop of mayo or sweet chilli dip on the side. If you want to keep things lighter, try them with a crunchy slaw or pile them into a wrap with lettuce and sauce for an easy homemade chicken wrap.

Puff Pastry Pie Top

 PREP TIME 5 MINUTES

 COOK TIME 12 MINUTES

 SERVES – FLEXIBLE: MAKES 1 LARGE OR SEVERAL SMALLER TOPS

1 320 g / 11 oz sheet ready-rolled puff pastry
1 small egg, beaten (for egg wash)

SAVOURY OPTION
Sprinkle with sesame seeds or poppy seeds before air frying

SWEET OPTION
Sprinkle with demerara sugar or a cinnamon–sugar mix for a caramelized finish, perfect over stewed apples or berries

Whether you're topping a hearty stew or finishing off some stewed fruit, a puff pastry lid is such an easy way to add a golden, flaky finish. It's quick, simple and works just as well for savoury or sweet pies – the air fryer gets it puffed and golden in no time.

1. Cut the puff pastry sheet to the size or shape you need for your pie top.

2. Use a knife to gently score the surface with a pattern of your choice – this makes the pastry look even more appealing once baked. Brush with egg wash and add your sweet or savoury toppings, if using.

3. Transfer to the air fryer drawer and cook at 180°C for 12 minutes, until golden and puffed.

TIP

If you don't need the whole sheet at once, cut the pastry into your preferred sizes and freeze them between sheets of baking paper. That way you can just grab a portion whenever you need it. Defrost before cooking for the best results. Much more useful than freezing the whole roll!

Quick Southern-fried Chicken Thighs

 PREP TIME 10 MINUTES

 COOK TIME 20 MINUTES

 SERVES 2

These are so crispy, you'd swear they were deep-fried. Juicy, golden and full of flavour, they're one of my go-tos when I want something that feels a bit indulgent but is still easy to throw together. Way quicker than the bone-in version – and just as good!

4 tbsp plain flour
1 medium egg, beaten
6 tbsp Southern-fried breadcrumbs
4 boneless, skinless chicken thighs (approx. 130 g / 4½ oz each)
Oil spray
Salt and pepper

1. You'll need three medium-sized bowls: add the plain flour to one bowl (season with salt and pepper), the beaten egg to another, and the breadcrumbs to the final bowl.

2. Coat each chicken thigh in the flour first (and shake off the excess), then dip into the egg and finally into the breadcrumbs until evenly coated.

3. Place the chicken thighs in a single layer in the air fryer drawer and spray liberally with oil – we want them nice and crispy!

4. Air fry at 190°C for 20 minutes, flipping halfway through and spraying again for extra crunch.

TIP

Serve with corn-on-the-cob for a proper Southern-style meal – just pop the corn in the air fryer for 12 minutes at 190°C, if you've got space, or boil or oven-bake it until tender. Add a dollop of coleslaw or some wedges on the side and you're sorted.

Honey & Mustard Pork Chops

 PREP TIME 5 MINUTES

 COOK TIME 15 MINUTES

 SERVES 2

Sticky, sweet and full of flavour, these honey and mustard pork chops are such a simple way to make dinner feel a bit special. The garlic adds a punchy depth, and the glaze turns golden and caramelized in the air fryer.

4 tbsp honey
4 tsp wholegrain mustard
2 garlic cloves, crushed
4 pork chops, boneless

TO SERVE
Mashed potato
Wilted spinach
Truffle oil (optional)

1. In a small bowl, mix together the honey, mustard and garlic.

2. Pour the mixture over your pork chops and rub in until evenly coated all over.

3. Transfer the pork chops to the air fryer drawer and pour over any of the remaining sauce.

4. Air fry for 15 minutes at 200°C, turning over after 10 minutes.

5. Once finished, plate up the mashed potato and wilted spinach, then top with the pork chops and pour over the juices from the air fryer. Finish with a drizzle of truffle oil if you're feeling fancy.

TIP

Honey can get sticky fast, especially in the heat of the air fryer. Once you've dished up, fill the drawer with warm soapy water and let it soak while you eat. It makes the clean-up way easier later.

Sausage Meatball Pasta Bake

 PREP TIME 10 MINUTES

 COOK TIME 18–20 MINUTES

 SERVES 2

160 g / 5½ oz dried rigatoni pasta (or similar)
6 good-quality sausages (400 g / 14 oz)
100 g / 3½ oz frozen petit pois peas
1 jar pasta sauce (350–400 g / 12–14 oz)
75 g / 2½ oz mature Cheddar cheese, grated

This is my go-to when I want comfort food with minimal faff! Using sausages instead of traditional meatballs is such a handy shortcut, and the result is just as tasty. It's a hearty, satisfying dish that's easy to prep and even better the next day.

1. Bring a pan of water to the boil and cook the pasta according to the packet instructions. Drain and set aside once done.

2. While the pasta is cooking, remove the skins from the sausages and split and roll each one into four equal pieces to make mini meatballs. I find the easiest way is to twist each sausage at both ends until the filling pops out.

3. Place the sausage meatballs into your air fryer basket and cook at 190°C for 10 minutes, giving them a shake halfway through.

4. Add the frozen peas to a bowl, pour over with boiling water and cover with a plate. Leave to sit for 5 minutes, then drain.

5. Once everything is prepped, add the pasta, peas and sausage meatballs to an air fryer-friendly dish (silicone dishes work really well). Stir through the jar of pasta sauce and top with a generous handful of cheese.

6. Air fry at 190°C for 8–10 minutes, until the top is golden, bubbling and slightly crispy.

MAIN MEALS

TIP

Switch up the flavour by using different types of sausage – herby, spicy, or even chicken – and stir in any leftover veg you've got in the fridge to bulk it out even more.

Lamb Chops with Minted Pea Mash

- PREP TIME 10 MINUTES
- COOK TIME 8 MINUTES
- SERVES 2

Lamb and mint is such a classic combo, and this version keeps it simple but full of flavour. The chops come out tender and pink, while the minted pea mash adds a herby, slightly sweet twist. It's a brilliant dinner for when you want something hearty without loads of prep.

4 lamb chops
Oil spray
75 g / 2½ oz frozen peas
400 g / 14 oz mashed potatoes, heated up (equivalent of 600 g / approx. 1 lb white potatoes or 4 medium potatoes if cooking from scratch)
2 tbsp mint sauce
Salt and pepper

1. Remove the lamb chops from the fridge and allow to sit at room temperature for 10 minutes.

2. Spray the chops with oil and season with salt and pepper on both sides.

3. Place the chops in the air fryer and cook for 8 minutes at 190°C, flipping halfway through.

4. While the lamb cooks, add the frozen peas to a bowl, pour over boiling water and cover with a plate. Leave for 5 minutes, then drain. Mash slightly with a fork and stir into the hot mashed potatoes along with the mint sauce.

5. Once the lamb is cooked, transfer to a chopping board, pour over the juices from the air fryer drawer, cover loosely with foil and rest for 5–10 minutes.

6. Divide the minted pea mash between two plates, top each with two lamb chops, spoon over the resting juices and enjoy.

TIP

For well-done, add a minute or two to the cooking time. For pinker meat, shave off a minute. Delicious served with carrots for an extra touch of sweetness.

Marmite Macaroni Cheese

 PREP TIME 5 MINUTES

 COOK TIME 25 MINUTES

 SERVES 2

I saw a recipe once for Creamy Air Fryer Mac and Cheese on the My Forking Life website that used uncooked macaroni, and I couldn't wait to give it a go. I love the fact that it's a throw-it-all-in kind of dish, and over the years I've adapted it into the most indulgent, delicious version with Marmite undertones and crispy bacon bits. It's rich, comforting and seriously tasty – perfect with a fresh green salad on the side.

MAIN MEALS

150 g / 5 oz macaroni (uncooked)
200 g / 7 oz mature Cheddar cheese, grated
1 tsp Marmite
120 ml / 4 fl oz whipping cream
1 tsp mustard powder
Salt & pepper

TO SERVE
Crispy bacon bits (optional)

1. Add the uncooked macaroni to an air fryer-friendly dish, along with three-quarters of the cheese.

2. In a jug, mix the Marmite into 240 ml / 8½ fl oz boiling water until dissolved.

3. Tip the Marmite water into the pan with the macaroni and cheese, then mix through your whipping cream and mustard powder. Season with salt and pepper.

4. Place the dish in the air fryer and air fry for 25 minutes at 180°C, stirring every 5 minutes.

5. When there are 10 minutes of cooking time left, sprinkle the remaining cheese on top and pat down with the back of a spoon to stop it from blowing around in the air fryer.

6. Once the cooking time is up, remove the pan from the air fryer and leave to cool for 10 minutes. The macaroni will thicken up during this time.

7. Sprinkle over the crispy bacon bits (if using).

Veggie option: Remove the bacon.

We all know you're either a lover or a hater of Marmite (I'm obviously a lover!), but if it's not your thing, just leave it out. It's still 10/10 without it.

Chicken Parmesan Schnitzel

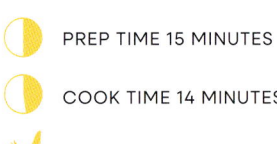

- PREP TIME 15 MINUTES
- COOK TIME 14 MINUTES
- SERVES 2

MAIN MEALS

This is pure comfort food – super-crispy, golden chicken with a garlicky Parmesan crumb that locks in flavour. It's quick to throw together but feels like a proper treat (and the bashing of the chicken is quite satisfying after a long day!). I love serving it with crispy new potatoes and some crunchy coleslaw, but it's just as good with a simple green salad if you're after something lighter.

2 chicken breasts (approx. 160 g / 5½ oz each)
40 g / 1½ oz plain flour
½ tsp garlic granules
½ tsp paprika
1 egg
50 g / 1¾ oz panko breadcrumbs
25 g / ¾ oz grated Parmesan
Oil spray
Salt and pepper

TO SERVE
Crispy new potatoes
Coleslaw

1. Trim any excess fat from the chicken breasts. Place each one in a plastic ziplock bag and bash with a rolling pin until around ½ cm / 1/4 inch thick. Leave them whole or cut into smaller schnitzels.

2. Line up three bowls: add your plain flour to one, along with the garlic granules and paprika, and season with salt and pepper; crack and beat an egg in the second bowl; add your panko breadcrumbs and Parmesan to the third bowl and stir to combine.

3. Coat each chicken piece in the flour, then dip into the egg, and finally press into the breadcrumb–Parmesan mix until fully coated.

4. Place the schnitzels in the air fryer drawer. Spray liberally with oil and cook at 200°C for 14 minutes, flipping halfway through and spraying again, until golden and cooked through.

5. Serve straight away with crispy new potatoes and coleslaw.

TIP

If you fancy a bit of sauce, a drizzle of garlic butter goes down nicely. And if you have leftovers, slice it up and enjoy with coleslaw and salad in a wrap the next day for lunch.
Why not take your crispy new potatoes to the next level by mixing them with some spring onion, lemon and olive oil.

Burger Tacos

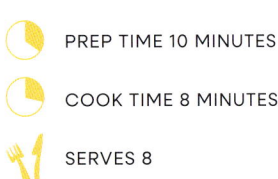

PREP TIME 10 MINUTES

COOK TIME 8 MINUTES

SERVES 8

These are such a crowd-pleaser! A mash-up of tacos and cheeseburgers that cook up brilliantly in the air fryer. The meat crisps at the edges, the cheese melts to golden loveliness, and the toppings bring that classic burger hit. They're seriously addictive and perfect for Friday nights, or even as a fun midweek dinner.

500 g / 1 lb beef mince
8 mini tortilla wraps
1 tbsp ketchup
1 tbsp mayonnaise
1 tbsp yellow mustard
8 cheese slices
Oil spray
Salt and pepper

TO SERVE
Gherkins, sliced
1 white onion, chopped
Tomatoes, sliced
Iceberg lettuce, finely sliced

1. Add the mince to a large bowl, season with salt and pepper, and mix together.

2. Divide the mince into eight equal portions.

3. Place one mini wrap on a board, top with a portion of mince and press down to spread the meat evenly across the wrap. Repeat with the remaining wraps.

4. Place the wraps in a single layer in your air fryer drawer (you may need to cook in batches), spray lightly with oil and air fry for 8 minutes at 190°C.

5. While they cook, mix together the ketchup, mayo and mustard in a small bowl to make your burger sauce.

6. When there's 1 minute left, pause the air fryer and pop a cheese slice on top of each taco.

7. Once cooked, serve up with a drizzle of sauce, gherkins (a must!), chopped onion, tomato slices and shredded lettuce. Tuck in!

TIP

You can mix things up with your favourite burger toppings – think crispy bacon, jalapeños or even a fried egg. They're great for kids, too – just let them build their own with whatever they like.

Super Simple Lamb Koftas

 PREP TIME 10 MINUTES

 COOK TIME 10 MINUTES

 SERVES 3

Tasty little fakeaway! These juicy lamb koftas are packed with flavour and super simple to throw together. They work brilliantly on skewers if you've bought yourself an air fryer rack with skewers, but if not, just shape them into sausages and cook them straight in the drawer. Quick, easy and properly satisfying.

MAIN MEALS

500 g / 1 lb lamb mince
1 tsp ground cumin
2 tsp ground coriander
2 tsp lazy garlic (pre-chopped or puréed)
1 tbsp chopped mint
Oil spray
Salt and pepper

TO SERVE
3 flatbreads
3 tbsp tzatziki
3 medium tomatoes, chopped
1 handful diced cucumber
1 handful chooped coriander
1 handful chopped mint

1. Add the lamb mince, spices, garlic, mint and a good pinch of salt and pepper to a mixing bowl. Use your hands to mix everything together really well.

2. Divide the mixture into three even portions and shape into sausage-like koftas.

3. Thread onto skewers (if you've got them) and give each one a gentle squeeze so they stay secure.

4. Pop onto your air fryer rack, spray with a little oil and air fry at 180°C for 10 minutes.

5. Once cooked, serve up in warm flatbreads with a spoonful of tzatziki, chopped tomato, cucumber and fresh coriander and mint.

TIP

Fancy a change from tzatziki? Try serving with hummus and a crumble of feta for a delicious twist. You could also add some pickled red onions or chilli sauce for extra flavour.

Thai Turkey Burgers

- PREP TIME 8 MINUTES
- COOK TIME 14 MINUTES
- SERVES 2

These are flavour-packed and absolutely delicious! Juicy turkey burgers loaded with Thai red curry paste, lime and coriander – they're quick to mix up, super fragrant and a refreshing change from your standard burger. Add that creamy, crunchy slaw on top and you've got a seriously satisfying bite.

250 g / 8¾ oz turkey mince
1½ tbsp Thai red curry paste
2 spring onions, finely chopped
½ tsp ginger paste
Zest of ½ lime
Small handful chopped coriander
1 tbsp panko breadcrumbs (optional, helps bind)
Oil spray

FOR THE SLAW
50 g / 1¾ oz red or white cabbage, thinly sliced
1 small carrot (approx. 30 g / 1 oz), grated or thinly ribboned
20 g / ¾ oz roasted peanuts, chopped
2 tbsp mayonnaise
½ tbsp sweet chilli sauce
Juice of ½ lime

TO SERVE
2 brioche buns (the ones with sesame seeds are best!)
Mayonnaise
Lettuce (optional)

1. In a bowl, combine the turkey mince, curry paste, spring onions, ginger, lime zest, coriander and breadcrumbs.

2. Shape into two evenly sized burger patties, slightly larger than your burger buns (they shrink a little when cooking).

3. Spray your air fryer crisper plate with a little oil to prevent sticking. Place the burgers on top, spray lightly with oil and air fry at 190°C for 14 minutes, flipping halfway, until golden and cooked through.

4. Meanwhile, prepare the slaw. Mix the cabbage, carrot and peanuts in one bowl. In another, stir together the mayo, sweet chilli sauce and lime juice, then combine everything and set aside.

5. Toast the brioche buns in the air fryer for 2 minutes at 190°C, or in a toaster until golden.

6. To build, spread a little mayo on the base of each bun, add lettuce, then the burger, top with the crunchy slaw and finish with the bun lid.

TIP

If you like a little extra kick, add a squeeze of sriracha or a spoon of chilli mayo on top before serving – it pairs perfectly with the slaw.

Prosciutto-wrapped Fish with Pesto & Asparagus

 PREP TIME 5 MINUTES

 COOK TIME 15–17 MINUTES

 SERVES 2

This one's quick to throw together but feels like a proper treat. Flaky white fish wrapped in salty prosciutto, with a spoonful of pesto and tender asparagus tucked inside – it's simple, full of flavour and a great option when you want something that feels a bit more special but still takes less than 20 minutes.

MAIN MEALS

6 slices prosciutto or Parma ham
2 × 125 g / 4 oz white fish fillets (like cod, haddock or basa)
4 tsp red pesto
10 asparagus tips

TO SERVE
Green salad
Cooked potatoes (optional)

1. Lay three slices of prosciutto overlapping on a board. Place one fish fillet in the centre, spoon over 2 teaspoons of red pesto, and top with the five asparagus tips.

2. Wrap the prosciutto around the fish and veg to form a tight parcel. Repeat with the second fillet.

3. Place both parcels in the air fryer and cook at 180°C for 15–17 minutes, until the fish is cooked through and the prosciutto is slightly crisped.

4. Serve with green salad, pour over the juices from the air fryer and tuck in.

TIP

You can swap the red pesto for green, or even a layer of soft cheese with herbs. It also works really well with salmon if you've got that in the fridge instead. You can prep the parcels a few hours ahead, keep them in the fridge, and cook when ready.
This dish is also lovely with some mixed grains and veg.

Salmon & Asparagus with Curried Potatoes & Chickpeas

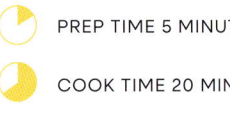

PREP TIME 5 MINUTES

COOK TIME 20 MINUTES

SERVES 2

This one is full of flavour and works brilliantly in a dual-drawer air fryer. The curry paste gives the potatoes and chickpeas loads of depth, and cooking the salmon over the asparagus means everything's done at once. Are you using a single drawer? Simply cook the potatoes and chickpeas for 10 minutes first, then add the salmon and asparagus on top (either on a rack or directly over the mix).

1 tin peeled potatoes
1 tin chickpeas
2 tbsp curry paste (I like to use Keralan curry paste)
1 pack asparagus tips
Garlic-infused oil
2 salmon fillets (approx. 120 g / 4 oz each)
Salt and pepper

1. Drain the potatoes and chickpeas, add to a bowl and mix together with the curry paste. Tip the mixture into one of the air fryer drawers.

2. Add the asparagus to the second drawer, drizzle with a little of the garlic oil and season with salt and pepper.

3. Add a rack over the asparagus and place the salmon fillets on the rack (skin side up). Drizzle the salmon skin with a little more of the garlic oil and season with salt and pepper (this will result in a lovely crispy skin – my favourite bit!).

4. Place both drawers in the air fryer. Select the 'Air fry' mode and set the salmon/asparagus for 10 minutes at 200°C and the potatoes/chickpeas for 20 minutes at 200°C – then select 'Sync' to finish so everything is ready at the same time. Give the potatoes/chickpeas a stir halfway through to ensure even cooking.

5. To serve, divide the potatoes/chickpeas mixture between two plates, followed by the asparagus, and then salmon fillets.

TIP

If you don't have tinned potatoes, you can use fresh baby potatoes instead, you'll just need to boil or microwave them until tender before mixing with the curry paste. You can also swap the asparagus for green beans or tenderstem broccoli, depending on what you've got.

Breaded Prawn Tacos with Sweet Chilli & Lime Mayo

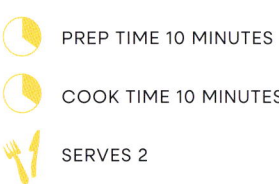

PREP TIME 10 MINUTES

COOK TIME 10 MINUTES

SERVES 2

I've made loads of prawn tacos over the years, but this version has become a favourite. The garlic-and-herb crumb adds loads of flavour, and the sweet chilli and lime mayo gives it a proper zing. It's quick, fresh and full of texture – think crispy prawns, creamy avocado and crunchy cabbage, all wrapped up in a warm, soft tortilla. Perfect for a weekend fakeaway or an easy dinner when you want something with a bit of a kick.

2 tbsp plain flour
1 medium egg
4 tbsp garlic-and-herb breadcrumbs
1 pack raw king prawns (roughly 170 g / 6 oz)
Oil spray
2 tbsp mayonnaise
1 tbsp sweet chilli sauce
½ lime (juice and a little zest)
4 small tortilla wraps
¼ red cabbage, finely shredded
1 avocado, sliced or smashed
3 spring onions, sliced
Handful chopped coriander
Salt and pepper

TO SERVE
Lime wedges

1. Set up three bowls. In the first, add the plain flour and season with salt and pepper. In the second, beat the egg. In the third, add the garlic-and-herb breadcrumbs.

2. Coat the prawns in flour, dip into the egg, then coat in the breadcrumbs until fully covered.

3. Place the prawns in the air fryer drawer and spray lightly with oil. Air fry at 200°C for 10 minutes, flipping and spraying again halfway through.

4. While the prawns are cooking, mix together the mayonnaise, sweet chilli sauce and a squeeze of lime juice in a small bowl. Add a little lime zest if you like.

5. Warm the tortilla wraps in the microwave for 20 seconds until soft.

6. To assemble, add a spoonful of red cabbage and avocado to each wrap, top with 3–4 prawns, a drizzle of the sweet chilli and lime mayo, spring onions and fresh coriander.

7. Serve with extra lime wedges and enjoy while everything is hot and crispy.

TIP

Swap the prawns for frozen ones, if that's what you've got – just defrost them first and pat dry before coating. Or, the prawns can be swapped for chunks of white fish, like cod or haddock, for an easy fish taco twist.

Sticky Teriyaki Salmon Traybake

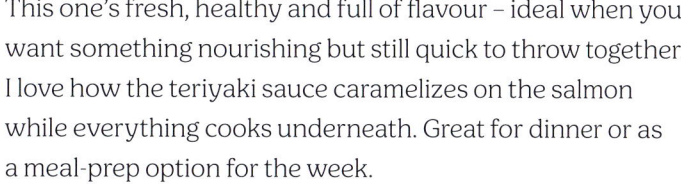

 PREP TIME 5 MINUTES

 COOK TIME 12–15 MINUTES

 SERVES 2

This one's fresh, healthy and full of flavour – ideal when you want something nourishing but still quick to throw together. I love how the teriyaki sauce caramelizes on the salmon while everything cooks underneath. Great for dinner or as a meal-prep option for the week.

100 g / 3½ oz tenderstem broccoli
100 g / 3½ oz green beans, trimmed
1 medium carrot, peeled and cut into thin batons or ribbons
100 g / 3½ oz frozen edamame beans (defrosted)
1 tsp sesame oil
2 salmon fillets (approx. 120 g / 4 oz each)
100–150 ml / 3½–5 fl oz teriyaki sauce
Salt and pepper

TO SERVE
1 spring onion, finely sliced
Toasted sesame seeds
A few sprigs of fresh coriander
Lime wedges (optional)

1. In a bowl, toss together the broccoli, green beans, carrot batons and defrosted edamame with the sesame oil, a pinch of salt and some black pepper.

2. Tip the veg mixture into the air fryer drawer and place the salmon fillets on top, skin side up.

3. Pour the teriyaki sauce on top of the salmon skin. (I use a pastry brush to evenly distribute the sauce across the salmon.)

4. Air fry at 200°C for 12 minutes. The veg will be al dente by this point, but if you prefer it softer, remove the salmon, shake the veg, and return it to the air fryer for another 3–5 minutes.

5. Plate up the veg, top with the salmon, and finish with spring onion, toasted sesame seeds and fresh coriander. If you fancy it, you could also add lime wedges for a fresh, zesty hit.

TIP

If your salmon fillets are quite thick, you might want to add an extra minute or two of cook time. And don't be afraid to switch up the veg based on what you've got in the fridge – pak choi, peppers or sugar snaps will all work brilliantly.

Prawn Air Fry

PREP TIME 5 MINUTES
COOK TIME 13 MINUTES
SERVES 2

This is one of my favourite midweek dinners. I usually grab one of those stir-fry meal deals from the supermarket (M&S do a good one) and just add an extra pack of sauce to bring it all together. Juicy prawns, fresh veg and noodles – quick, tasty, and it all cooks in one go. Also delicious cold for lunch the next day!

1 pack stir-fry veg
Oil spray
1 pack cooked noodles
2 packs of stir-fry sauce
1 pack raw king prawns

TO SERVE
1 spring onion, finely sliced

1. Start by removing the crisper tray from your air fryer drawer and tip in the veg.

2. Spray with oil, stir together and air fry for 5 minutes at 190°C.

3. After the 5 minutes is up, add the noodles and one packet of sauce, stir and air fry for another 3 minutes at 190°C.

4. Meanwhile, add the prawns to a bowl and mix in the second packet of sauce.

5. Prepare the prawns on skewers (most air fryer racks come with skewers).

6. Once the veg and noodles are done, add the rack to the air fryer, over the veg/noodles, and add the prawns skewers to the rack. If you don't have skewers, you can lay the prawns on top of the rack.

7. Air fry everything for a final 5 minutes at 190°C, until the prawns are pink and cooked through. If you've laid them directly on top rather than using skewers, give them an extra 2 minutes to make sure they're cooked through. Garnish with spring onion.

TIP

Most air fryer racks come with skewers – this is a great chance to actually use them. If you don't have any, you can just place the prawns straight onto the rack or mix them into the noodles at the end.

Tuna & Cheese Loaded Potato Skins

 PREP TIME 10 MINUTES

 COOK TIME 15 MINUTES

 SERVES 2

These are such a great way to use up leftover jacket potatoes and turn a tin of tuna into something proper tasty. Crispy on the outside, soft and cheesy in the middle – they're quick to throw together and brilliant for lunch or an easy weeknight dinner. I always have these ingredients knocking about, so they've become a bit of a go-to.

MAIN MEALS

2 jacket potatoes
1 tin of tuna
50 g / 1¾ oz mature Cheddar cheese, grated, plus extra for topping
2 spring onions, sliced, plus extra for sprinkling
2 tbsp mayonnaise
Zest of 1 lemon
Salt and pepper

1. Slice the potatoes in half and scrape out the middle into a bowl, being careful not to break the skins. Mash the potato with a fork, then add the tuna, cheese, spring onions, mayonnaise and lemon zest. Season with salt and pepper and mix everything together.

2. Spoon the filling back into the potato skins, patting it down with the back of a fork so you can pack in as much as possible!

3. Top with a little extra cheese and spring onion, transfer to your air fryer drawer and cook for 15 minutes at 190°C - until golden and bubbling.

TIP

Delicious served with a simple salad. I love them with salad cream or sweet chilli sauce, depending on what else is on the plate!

Crispy Fish Burgers with Homemade Tartare Sauce

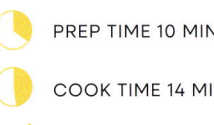

PREP TIME 10 MINUTES

COOK TIME 14 MINUTES

SERVES 2

When I was a teenager, my order from McDonald's was always the Filet-O-Fish, so of course I had to recreate it in the air fryer! This version does not disappoint … it's proper comfort food.

2 tbsp plain flour
1 egg, beaten
4 tbsp breadcrumbs (I like to mix panko and golden breadcrumbs, but use whatever you have!)
260 g / 9 oz white fish fillets (approx. 2 × 130 g / 4.5 oz, skinless and boneless)
Oil spray
Salt and pepper

FOR THE TARTARE SAUCE
2 tbsp mayonnaise
1 tsp lemon juice
1 tsp capers, chopped
2 gherkin slices, finely chopped
Small handful chopped parsley
Black pepper

TO SERVE
2 brioche burger buns
2–4 cheese slices

1. Set up your coating station with three bowls: one with seasoned flour, one with the beaten egg and one with the mixed breadcrumbs.

2. Pat the fish dry with kitchen roll and then dip each fillet into the flour, then into the egg, and finally into the breadcrumbs. For an extra-crispy crust, dip again into the egg and then back into the breadcrumbs.

3. Spray the air fryer crisper tray lightly with oil. Add the fish fillets in a single layer, spray lightly with oil and air fry at 190°C for 14 minutes, flipping halfway through and spraying again with oil.

4. While the fish is cooking, make your tartare sauce. Stir together the mayo, lemon juice, capers, gherkins, parsley and a crack of black pepper.

5. Pop the brioche buns into the air fryer for the final minute of cooking time to warm through, or if you don't have room, pop them in a toaster to toast lightly.

6. To assemble, spoon tartare sauce onto the base of each bun, top with a slice of cheese, the crispy fish, another slice of cheese (optional!), and a little more tartare sauce on the top bun. Pop the lid on and tuck in!

TIP

If your fish fillets are on the thicker side, add an extra minute or two to the cook time – this recipe is based on fillets around 2.5 cm / 1 inch thick. I serve these with skinny fries and crunchy slaw!

Miso-glazed Fish with Sticky Rice & Greens

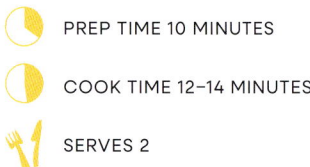

PREP TIME 10 MINUTES

COOK TIME 12–14 MINUTES

SERVES 2

This one feels fancy but is super easy to throw together. The miso glaze gives the fish loads of flavour, and the whole thing cooks together in the air fryer – rice, greens and all. It's light, packed with umami, and comes together in under 15 minutes.

100 g / 3½ oz frozen peas
2 skinless white fish fillets (cod, haddock or basa, approx. 120–140 g / 4–4¾ oz each)
250 g / 8½ oz pouch microwaveable jasmine rice
2 spring onions, sliced
1 small head pak choi, leaves separated
1 tsp sesame seeds
1 small red chilli, finely sliced (optional)

FOR THE MARINADE/SAUCE
1 tbsp white miso paste
1 tbsp light soy sauce
1 tsp sesame oil
1 tsp honey, plus extra for drizzling
1 tsp garlic and ginger paste
Black pepper

1. Add the frozen peas to a bowl, pour over with boiling water and cover with a plate. Leave to sit for 5 minutes, then drain.

2. Meanwhile, make the marinade. In a shallow, medium-sized dish, mix the miso paste, soy sauce, sesame oil, honey, garlic and ginger paste, and a good crack of black pepper.

3. Place the fish fillets in the dish and coat with the marinade. Cover and chill for a couple of hours if you have time – if not, move straight on.

4. Remove the crisper plate from the air fryer drawer. Tip in the rice (ensuring it's all broken up and not in one big clump straight out of the packet!), peas and spring onions and mix together.

5. Place the rack over the rice mixture, then lay the pak choi in a criss-cross pattern on top of the rack, followed by the marinated fish fillets. Spoon any leftover marinade over the top.

6. Air fry at 190°C for 12–14 minutes, until the fish is cooked through and flaky.

7. Remove the fish carefully, lift out the rack, then stir the veg and rice to coat them in all the lovely sauce and juices.

8. Plate up the rice and greens, top with the fish, sprinkle with sesame seeds and sliced chilli (if using).

TIP

This works best with a rack to keep air circulating between the rice and pak choi/fish. If you don't have one, place the veg and fish directly on top of the rice. Once it's finished, remove the fish/veg, give the rice a stir and pop the rice back in for 1 minute at 180°C.

No pak choi? Try green beans, broccoli, or sliced courgette – just aim for quick-cooking veg.

Lemon Garlic Butter Prawns with Linguine

 PREP TIME 5 MINUTES

 COOK TIME 9 MINUTES

 SERVES 2

This dish is inspired by a favourite meal I used to order whenever I visited Florida – a simple but delicious combination of prawns, garlic, butter and lemon. My version uses the air fryer and a quick toss through pasta to bring all those flavours home in an easy weeknight dinner. If you don't fancy pasta, it's just as good served with some crusty bread and butter to soak up all the garlicky sauce.

MAIN MEALS

30 g / 1 oz unsalted butter
2 garlic cloves, minced, or 1 tsp lazy garlic (pre-chopped or puréed)
Zest of ½ lemon
1 tbsp lemon juice
165 g / 6 oz pack of raw king prawns
150 g / 5 oz pasta (linguine or spaghetti work well)
1 tsp grated Parmesan, plus extra to serve
1 tbsp chopped parsley
Black pepper

1. Place the butter and garlic in an air fryer-friendly dish that fits inside your drawer (large enough to hold the prawns). Air fry at 180°C for 2 minutes until the butter has melted and the garlic is fragrant.

2. Add the lemon zest and juice and a crack of black pepper to the melted butter and stir to combine.

3. Pat the prawns dry with kitchen paper, then add them to the dish and toss until coated in the butter mixture.

4. Spread the prawns out in a single layer in the dish. Air fry at 190°C for 7 minutes, stirring halfway through, until the prawns are pink and cooked through.

5. Meanwhile, cook the pasta in a pan of boiling salted water according to the packet instructions.

6. Once the prawns are cooked, stir through the Parmesan and parsley. Add the drained pasta directly into the dish with the prawns and buttery sauce, tossing everything together until well coated.

7. Divide between two bowls, top with extra Parmesan, and serve immediately.

TIP

Start to cook your pasta just before the butter and garlic go into the air fryer so everything comes together at the same time. For extra flavour, add a pinch of smoked paprika or chilli flakes to the butter mixture.

Salmon en Croûte

 PREP TIME 10 MINUTES

 COOK TIME 20 MINUTES

 SERVES 2 GENEROUSLY (OR 4 WITH SIDES)

This is one of those meals that looks like you've made loads of effort, but it's actually really simple. The portions are generous too – you can serve two people from each one if you're adding sides, or just have the whole thing to yourself with some greens or a salad (depending on how hungry you are). Flaky pastry, creamy filling, perfectly cooked salmon ... what's not to love?

100 g / 3½ oz baby spinach
½ pack of Boursin cheese
1 320 g / 11 oz sheet ready-rolled puff pastry
2 skinless salmon fillets (approx. 120 g / 4 oz each)
1 small egg, beaten (for egg wash)
Black pepper

1. Add the baby spinach to a colander over a saucepan, pour over boiling water and leave to wilt for 5 minutes. Once the 5 minutes have passed, use the back of a spoon to squeeze out as much water as possible from the spinach.

2. Once the spinach has cooled slightly, chop up and mix in the Boursin and season with black pepper, then set to one side.

3. Lay out the puff pastry, place the two salmon fillets at the bottom of the pastry so there's equal distance around them, and separate out the spinach mixture on top of the fillets.

4. Cut the pastry in half, both lengthways and widthways, so you have four even slices.

5. Brush the pastry around the salmon fillets with the beaten egg, then place the other slices of pastry on top.

6. Use the back of a fork to seal all the way around the edge of the pastry and prick the top so the steam releases during cooking.

7. Transfer both of the en croûte fillets to the air fryer, brush with egg, and air fry for 20 minutes at 180°C.

TIP

If you don't have Boursin, you can use garlic and herb cream cheese or even a little pesto mixed with soft cheese. You can also swap the spinach for cooked leeks, if that's what you've got to hand!

Cheesy Cauliflower Steaks

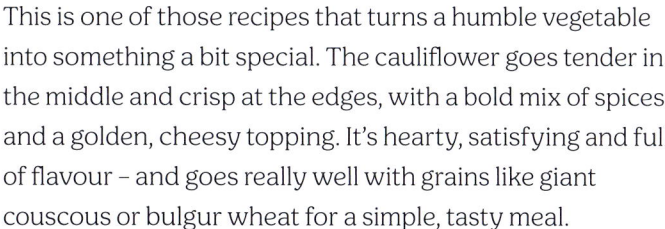

 PREP TIME 5 MINUTES

 COOK TIME 24 MINUTES

 SERVES 2

This is one of those recipes that turns a humble vegetable into something a bit special. The cauliflower goes tender in the middle and crisp at the edges, with a bold mix of spices and a golden, cheesy topping. It's hearty, satisfying and full of flavour – and goes really well with grains like giant couscous or bulgur wheat for a simple, tasty meal.

1 cauliflower
2 tbsp oil
1 tsp paprika
½ tsp garlic granules
½ tsp onion granules
½ tsp ground cumin
½ tsp chilli flakes
100 g / 3½ oz mature Cheddar cheese, grated
Salt and pepper

1. Slice the base off the cauliflower to remove the leaves, then cut into 2–3 cm- /¾–1¼ inch-thick steaks. You'll get two or three good ones from the middle, and you can save the smaller bits for another day (or use them in the Bang Bang Cauliflower recipe on page 157).

2. In a small bowl, mix together the oil, paprika, garlic granules, onion granules, cumin, chilli flakes, salt and pepper.

3. Add a paper liner to your air fryer drawer if you have one (not essential, just helps with the clean-up). Lay out the cauliflower steaks in an even layer.

4. Brush the cauliflower with half the spiced oil mixture, making sure you get into every nook and cranny!

5. Air fry at 190°C for 10 minutes.

6. Flip the steaks over, brush with the remaining oil mix, and cook for another 10 minutes at 190°C.

7. Sprinkle the grated cheese over the top and return to the air fryer for a final 4 minutes, until the cheese is melted and golden.

TIP

Vegan option: You can easily make this dairy-free by swapping the Cheddar for a plant-based cheese. Just make sure it's a variety that melts well for the best finish.

Mexican Rice-stuffed Peppers

 PREP TIME 10 MINUTES

 COOK TIME 20 MINUTES

 SERVES 3

A quick, easy and tasty midweek dinner! You can easily make this vegan by swapping in a plant-based cheese, or if you're not a veggie fan, add some cooked chicken if you want to bulk it out. Serve with salsa, guacamole or sour cream and you're sorted.

MAIN MEALS

3 red peppers
1 pack ready-cooked Mexican-style rice
2 spring onions, sliced
50 g / 1¾ oz mature Cheddar cheese, grated, plus extra for topping

TO SERVE
Salsa, guacamole, sour cream (optional)

1. Slice the tops off the peppers and carefully remove the stem, core and seeds.

2. Dice the tops of the peppers into small cubes and add to a bowl with the rice, sliced spring onions and grated cheese. Mix everything together.

3. Spoon the mixture into the peppers and top with a little extra cheese.

4. Place the stuffed peppers in the air fryer drawer and cook at 180°C for 20 minutes, until the peppers have softened and the cheese is melted and golden.

5. Serve with your favourite dips – salsa, guacamole, sour cream, or all three!

TIP

Vegan option: This is a great one for using up leftovers. Swap the rice for couscous, quinoa or whatever grain you've got in the cupboard. You can also add black beans, sweetcorn or a spoonful of salsa to the filling for extra texture and flavour.

Pesto Parmesan Mushroom Pasta

 PREP TIME 5 MINUTES

 COOK TIME 15–17 MINUTES (DEPENDING ON THE SIZE OF THE MUSHROOMS)

 SERVES 2

2 large flat mushrooms
Oil spray
2 tbsp grated Parmesan, plus extra to serve
2 tbsp panko breadcrumbs
200 g / 7 oz dried pasta, to serve (spaghetti, tagliatelle or rigatoni all work well)
2 tbsp green pesto
Black pepper, to taste

This one's so simple, but so good. Juicy, meaty mushrooms cooked in the air fryer get topped with pesto and a crispy Parmesan-and-panko crust, then stirred through pasta for a veggie dish that's full of flavour and properly satisfying.

1. Remove the stalks from the mushrooms and place open side down in the air fryer drawer.

2. Spray the mushrooms with oil and air fry for 7 minutes at 170°C.

3. While the mushrooms are cooking, mix together the Parmesan cheese and panko breadcrumbs in a small bowl.

4. Cook your pasta as per the package instructions (normally 9–12 minutes).

5. Once the 7 minutes are up, turn the mushrooms over, then fill each with 1 tablespoon of pesto and divide the Parmesan-and-panko mixture between them.

6. Use the back of a spoon to pat down the Parmesan mixture so it doesn't blow around the air fryer.

7. Air fry for 8–10 minutes at 180°C until bubbling and golden.

8. Chop the cooked mushrooms into chunks and stir them through the pasta. Finish with a crack of black pepper and a sprinkle of extra Parmesan.

TIP

If you don't fancy pasta, the mushrooms work brilliantly on their own as a starter or side.

Boursin & Tomato Pasta

- PREP TIME 5 MINUTES
- COOK TIME 17 MINUTES
- SERVES 2

This is one of those viral recipes that actually lives up to the hype. I first saw it doing the rounds on social media and had to give it a go – now it's one of my go-to dinners when the fridge is looking a bit bare. It's creamy, garlicky, and full of flavour with barely any effort. Just throw everything in, cook your pasta, and you're done.

150 g / 5 oz block of Boursin, or similar
150 g / 5 oz cherry tomatoes
Oil spray
½ tsp garlic granules
1 tbsp chopped, fresh basil, plus extra to serve
200 g / 7 oz spaghetti
Salt and pepper

1. Place the Boursin and cherry tomatoes in an air fryer-friendly dish (I like to use the silicone liners for this). Spray the tomatoes with oil, season with salt and pepper and sprinkle with the garlic granules and fresh basil.

2. Air fry for 17 minutes at 190°C.

3. Meanwhile cook the spaghetti as per the packet instructions, normally for around 11 minutes.

4. Once the air fryer is finished, remove the dish and break down the tomatoes and Boursin with a fork and mix together until everything is combined.

5. Drain your pasta and tip in the Boursin and tomato sauce, then stir until the pasta is evenly coated.

6. Split between two bowls and finish with another sprinkle of basil.

TIP

If you want to bulk it out, add a handful of mushrooms before air frying, or serve with air-fried broccoli for a hit of green. Spray the broccoli with oil, season and cook at 200°C for 7–9 minutes until crispy, then add it to the dish when you mix through the pasta.

Halloumi Burger

 PREP TIME 10 MINUTES

 COOK TIME 15 MINUTES

 SERVES 2

A proper feel-good veggie burger. Crispy halloumi, sweet roasted red pepper and a messy but worth it combo of hummus and sweet chilli sauce (one of my faves!). This one is full of flavour and texture, quick to make and feels like a bit of a treat.

MAIN MEALS

225 g / 8 oz block halloumi
3 tbsp plain flour
1 egg
5 tbsp white breadcrumbs
1 red pepper
Oil spray
Salt and pepper

TO SERVE
2 brioche burger buns
4 tsp red pepper hummus
Sweet chilli sauce
Iceberg lettuce
Tomato slices
Cucumber slices

1. Slice the halloumi lengthways into two even pieces (you could stretch it to three if you prefer a thinner slice).

2. Set up three bowls. To the first, add the plain flour and season with salt and pepper. In the second, beat the egg. To the third, add the breadcrumbs.

3. Dip each slice of halloumi into the flour, then into the egg, then coat well in the breadcrumbs. Set aside.

4. Cut the red pepper in half and remove the stem and seeds.

5. Place the halloumi and red pepper halves into the air fryer drawer. A paper liner under the halloumi helps avoid sticking, but don't worry if you don't have one. Spray everything with oil.

6. Air fry at 190°C for 15 minutes, flipping halfway through.

7. For the final minute, warm the sliced brioche buns in the air fryer on a rack if you have one – or pop them in the toaster.

8. To build your burger, spread 1 teaspoon of red pepper hummus on the bottom bun and drizzle over a little sweet chilli sauce. Add a slice of red pepper, a halloumi slice, lettuce, tomato and cucumber, then spread another teaspoon of hummus on the top bun, sandwich it all together and get stuck in!

TIP

Want to switch it up? Try swapping the red pepper hummus for garlic hummus, or add a few slices of avocado for an extra creamy layer. This also works really well in a wrap if you're out of buns!

Baked Sweet Potato with Goat's Cheese & Sun-dried Tomatoes

 PREP TIME 10 MINUTES

 COOK TIME 30 MINUTES

 SERVES 2 AS A MAIN (OR AS 4 LIGHTER LUNCH PORTIONS WITH A SIDE SALAD)

Fluffy sweet potatoes baked in the air fryer, filled with a creamy goat's cheese, spinach and sun-dried tomato mix, then finished with crunchy walnuts and a drizzle of balsamic glaze. This makes a delicious main for two, or stretch it to four lighter portions with a side salad.

4 small sweet potatoes, approx. 120 g / 4 oz each
Oil spray
100 g / 3½ oz baby spinach
100 g / 3½ oz soft goat's cheese
40 g / 1½ oz sun-dried tomatoes, finely chopped
2 spring onions, finely sliced (or 1 if you don't want it too oniony!)
Salt and pepper

TO SERVE
Rocket
25 g / ¾ oz walnuts, roughly chopped
Balsamic glaze

1. Pierce the sweet potatoes a few times with a fork, spray with oil, season with salt and pepper, then place in the air fryer drawer. Air fry at 180°C for 25 minutes (depending on size) until soft in the middle and crispy on the outside.

2. While the potatoes cook, add the spinach to a colander over a saucepan. Pour over boiling water and leave for 5 minutes to wilt. After 5 minutes, press the spinach with the back of a spoon to squeeze out as much water as possible.

3. Add the goat's cheese, spinach, sun-dried tomatoes and spring onions to a mini chopper and blend until combined (or chop finely and stir together in a bowl).

4. When the sweet potatoes are ready, slice them in half lengthways. Place a liner in the air fryer drawer, arrange the sweet potato halves flesh side up, then spoon the goat's cheese mixture into each. Return to the air fryer at 190°C for 5 minutes until golden on top.

5. Serve with a rocket salad, scatter with walnuts and finish with a drizzle of balsamic glaze.

TIP

If your sweet potatoes are larger, give them an extra 5–10 minutes in the air fryer to make sure the centres are fluffy before filling. Alternatively, cut them in half lengthways before cooking.

If you're prepping lunches for the week ahead, this pairs really well with the Roasted Aubergine recipe on page 137 – they make a brilliant salad duo!

Gnocchi with Mushrooms, Spinach, Ricotta, Walnuts & Lemon

 PREP TIME 10 MINUTES

 COOK TIME 17 MINUTES

 SERVES 2–3 AS LARGE PORTIONS (OR 4 AS SMALLER ONES WITH A SIDE SALAD)

Bored of Lunch did a carbonara-style gnocchi in the air fryer and it was lovely! It inspired me to come up with my own version, and this one does not disappoint. The gnocchi soaks up all that gorgeous mushroom flavour, while the creamy ricotta, fresh spinach, toasted walnuts and hit of lemon bring it all together. Simple, satisfying and a little bit elegant!

200 g / 7 oz large flat mushrooms, sliced ½ cm thick
2 garlic cloves, crushed
500 g / 1 lb fresh gnocchi
Oil spray
100 g / 3½ oz baby spinach
50 g / 1¾ oz walnuts, roughly chopped
75 g / 2½ oz ricotta
50 g / 1¾ oz Parmesan, grated, plus extra to serve
Zest of ½ lemon, plus a squeeze of juice
Black pepper

1 Air fry the sliced mushrooms on the crisper tray at 190°C for 5 minutes.

2 Tip the mushrooms out and remove the crisper tray (the easiest way to do this is with some silicone tongs, as it'll be hot – don't burn those fingers!). Then add the mushrooms back into the drawer along with the garlic and gnocchi. Spray with oil, season with black pepper and air fry at 200°C for 12 minutes, shaking halfway.

3 Meanwhile, add the baby spinach to a colander over a saucepan. Pour over boiling water and leave for 5 minutes to wilt, and then use the back of a spoon to press out as much water as possible.

4 Toast the walnuts in a dry pan or in the air fryer for 3–4 minutes until golden and fragrant.

5 Once the gnocchi and mushrooms are cooked, stir through the ricotta, wilted spinach, Parmesan, lemon zest and a squeeze of juice. The heat from the drawer will bring everything together into a creamy sauce.

6 Serve immediately, topped with the toasted walnuts, extra Parmesan, black pepper and another squeeze of lemon to cut through the creaminess.

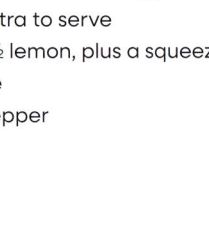

TIP

Swap the walnuts for toasted pine nuts, if you prefer, or add a drizzle of truffle oil to make it even more indulgent! You can also stir through some crispy chorizo or pancetta for a meaty twist. Delicious served with a simple side salad for a touch of freshness.

Broccoli Stalk Burgers

 PREP TIME 10 MINUTES

 COOK TIME 10–12 MINUTES

 SERVES 2

The perfect use for leftover stalks! I first saw chef Tristan Welch create a version of this idea and was inspired to see if it would work in the air fryer – and it really does. The result is a golden, savoury burger that's soft in the middle, lightly crisp at the edges and full of flavour. I love that it gives a second life to something we'd usually throw away.

MAIN MEALS

1 broccoli stalk (trim any woody bits)
10 g / ½ oz fresh chives, finely chopped
½ tsp harissa seasoning
1 tbsp plain flour
30 g / 1 oz feta, crumbled
1 egg yolk
Oil spray
Salt and pepper

TO SERVE
2 brioche buns, sliced
Favourite condiments

1. Grate the broccoli stalk and add to a bowl. Season with salt and pepper, then add the chives, harissa seasoning and flour. Mix well, then stir through the feta and egg yolk until combined.

2. Divide the mixture into two evenly sized portions and shape into burgers.

3. Place in the air fryer drawer, spray lightly with oil and cook at 180°C for 10–12 minutes, flipping halfway through, until golden and firm to the touch.

4. Add the brioche buns to the air fryer for the final minute to toast.

5. Build your burgers with your favourite condiments – I love mine with spicy mayo, tomato and gherkin – and dig in!

TIP

You can switch up the flavours depending on what you've got – try swapping feta for Cheddar or Parmesan, or add a spoonful of sweet chilli sauce to the mix for a little kick.

You only use the broccoli stalk here, but you could use the broccoli heads for some tasty Roasted Veggies – see page 147 for the recipe.

Roasted Aubergine with Herby Couscous & Harissa Yoghurt

 PREP TIME 5 MINUTES

 COOK TIME 20 MINUTES

 SERVES 2 AS A MAIN (OR 4 AS LIGHTER LUNCH PORTIONS WITH A SIDE SALAD)

Soft, caramelized aubergine halves served with fluffy, herby couscous and a dollop of cooling yoghurt swirled with harissa. Sweet pomegranate adds crunch, while crumbled feta brings creaminess. Big on flavour, super satisfying, and really easy to throw together!

MAIN MEALS

2 medium-sized aubergines
Oil spray
1 tsp smoked paprika
100 g / 3½ oz couscous
½ vegetable stock cube
1 handful fresh herbs (e.g. parsley, coriander, mint – whatever you have)
1 tbsp lemon juice
2 tbsp Greek yoghurt
1 tsp harissa paste
Salt and pepper

TO SERVE
50 g / 1¾ oz crumbled feta
80 g / 2¾ oz pomegranate seeds
Toasted nuts (optional, but pine nuts work really well)

1. Slice the aubergines in half lengthways and score the flesh in a criss-cross pattern – but don't cut all the way through. Spray with oil and season with salt, pepper and paprika.

2. Place the aubergine halves flesh side up in the air fryer. Air fry at 190°C for 20 minutes, flipping once the flesh has turned golden, soft and slightly caramelized.

3. Meanwhile, make the couscous: add the couscous and crumbled stock cube to a bowl, pour over 150 ml / 5 fl oz boiling water, cover with a plate and leave for 5 minutes. Fluff up with a fork, then stir through the chopped herbs and lemon juice.

4. Swirl the yoghurt and the harissa together in a bowl.

5. Spoon the couscous onto plates, then top with the roasted aubergine halves and a dollop of harissa yoghurt. Scatter over the feta, pomegranate seeds and toasted nuts (if using). Finish with a few extra herbs if you have them (looks and tastes good!).

TIP

Vegan option: Use vegan, dairy-free yoghurt and leave out the feta.

This is brilliant for advance lunch prep – make the aubergines and couscous ahead of time, then just add the yoghurt, feta and toppings when ready to eat.

Peanut Satay Veg Bao Buns

 PREP TIME 10 MINUTES

 COOK TIME 18 MINUTES

 SERVES 2

Soft, fluffy bao buns packed with charred veg and coated in a rich, creamy satay sauce – these are seriously satisfying. They're quick to make, full of flavour and perfect for when you want something a little different for lunch or dinner.

FOR THE FILLING
1 courgette, sliced into 1 cm / ½ inch strips
1 red pepper, deseeded and sliced into 1 cm / ½ inch strips
Oil spray
Salt and pepper

FOR THE SATAY SAUCE
2 tbsp smooth peanut butter
1 tbsp soy sauce
1 tsp sesame oil
1 tsp honey
Juice of ½ lime
1 garlic clove, finely grated (or ½ tsp garlic purée)

TO SERVE
4 bao buns (ready-to-steam or ready-to-heat)
Chopped spring onions
Crushed peanuts
Fresh coriander (optional)
Lime wedges

1. Add the sliced courgette and red pepper to a bowl. Spray with oil, season with salt and pepper, and toss to coat.

2. Transfer the veg to your air fryer drawer and air fry at 190°C for 18 minutes, shaking halfway through, until tender and crispy at the edges.

3. While the veg cook, make the satay sauce. In a small bowl, mix together the peanut butter, soy sauce, sesame oil, honey, lime juice and garlic. Add 1–2 tablespoons of warm water a little at a time until you have a smooth, spoonable sauce.

4. Once the vegetables are done, tip them into a bowl and pour over the satay sauce. Toss to coat evenly.

5. Warm the bao buns as per the pack instructions, then fill each one with the satay veg. Top with chopped spring onions, crushed peanuts and fresh coriander.

6. Serve immediately, with lime wedges for squeezing over the top.

Vegan option: Just leave out the honey – and make sure the bao buns are vegan-friendly too.

On the Side

Crispy Tandoori Baby Potatoes

ON THE SIDE

PREP TIME 5 MINUTES

COOK TIME 25–30 MINUTES

SERVES 4

These are full of flavour and couldn't be easier to make. Just a quick toss in tandoori spice and oil, then into the air fryer until they're golden and crisp on the outside, fluffily soft in the middle. They make a brilliant side dish, but I also love them as a snack with a dollop of mango chutney on the side. Total crowd-pleaser!

750 g / 1½ lb baby potatoes
Oil spray
2 tsp tandoori curry powder

TO SERVE
Mango chutney (optional)
Fresh coriander, finely chopped (optional)

1. Wash the potatoes, pat dry and cut any of the larger ones in half so they're all a similar size.

2. Place the potatoes in a bowl, spray liberally with oil and mix through the curry powder until everything is evenly coated.

3. Transfer the potatoes to the air fryer drawer and cook for 25–30 minutes at 200°C until crisp, golden and perfectly cooked.

4. Once cooked, transfer to a serving dish, then sprinkle with coriander and serve with a small bowl of the mango chutney (if using).

TIP

Try switching up the seasoning depending on what you're serving them with – garam masala, curry powder or even smoked paprika all work well. These also reheat nicely in the air fryer if you've got any left over.

Truffle Parmesan Fries

 PREP TIME 5 MINUTES

 COOK TIME 10–15 MINUTES

 SERVES 1

Crispy and packed with truffle flavour – these are next level. Probably the only time you'll see me cooking fries in the air fryer! The truffle oil adds richness, the Parmesan brings a salty, cheesy hit, and it all just works beautifully. Ideal as a side or a snack when you want something with a bit of wow.

2 large handfuls fresh or frozen skinny fries
Truffle oil
Fresh parsley, finely chopped
1 tbsp Parmesan, grated

TO SERVE
Aioli for dipping (optional)

1. Cook your fries as per the packet instructions – for skinny fries this is normally 10 minutes from fresh or 15 minutes from frozen at 200°C – and shake a couple of times throughout.

2. Once cooked, add to a bowl, drizzle with some truffle oil and sprinkle with a small handful of parsley and the grated Parmesan.

3. Mix everything together, serve with a little delicious aioli (if using) for dipping and enjoy!

These work best with skinny fries, but you can use chunky chips or wedges too – just adjust the cook time accordingly.

Garlic Peri Peri Wedges

 PREP TIME 5 MINUTES

 COOK TIME 20–25 MINUTES

 SERVES 2

Air fryer wedges come out spot-on every time – fluffy inside, crispy outside – and are way easier than oven-baking. A brilliant side for burgers, wraps or anything that needs a bit of crunch.

3 medium-sized white potatoes
Oil spray
2 tsp peri peri seasoning (vegan-friendly)
A sprinkle of garlic granules (you don't need a lot for a hit of flavour, go gently!)

1. Slice the potatoes into chunky wedges, about 2 cm / ¾ inch thick. Rinse with cold water, pat dry and place in a large bowl.

2. Spray liberally with oil and mix in the spices until evenly coated.

3. Transfer to the air fryer drawer in an even layer and air fry for 20–25 minutes at 190°C, shaking a couple of times throughout.

TIP

Be adventurous with seasonings – cajun spices, smoked paprika or garlic salt all work well, too.

Roasted Veggies

 PREP TIME 12 MINUTES

 COOK TIME 15–20 MINUTES

 SERVES 4

This is one of my go-to recipes for using up whatever veg I've got lying around. It's quick, flexible and perfect for batch-cooking. Just throw it all in the air fryer and let it do the work. If you're using harder veg like potatoes or butternut squash, give them a 5-minute head start before adding everything else so it all cooks evenly.

1 head of broccoli, cut into florets
2 carrots, sliced into 1 cm / ½ inch chunks
2 peppers, deseeded and sliced
1 red onion, peeled and cut into chunks
2 tbsp high-smoke-point oil (e.g. avocado, vegetable or sunflower oil)
1 tsp chilli flakes (or more if you like heat!)
Salt and pepper

1. Add all the vegetables to a large mixing bowl. Drizzle over the oil, season with salt and pepper, and sprinkle in the chilli flakes. Toss well to coat everything evenly.

2. Transfer the veg to your air fryer drawer in a single layer. Air fry at 180°C for 15–20 minutes, until the veg are cooked to your preference. Shake the drawer a few times throughout for even cooking.

3. Serve hot as a side, split into individual portions for lunches/dinners through the week, or mix into rice bowls, wraps or salads.

ON THE SDIE

TIP

Serve as a side, stir through rice or noodles, or portion it up for lunches through the week (the veggies will keep in the fridge in an airtight container for up to four days). I love these with couscous and a dollop of hummus for a super-quick dinner.

Honey & Feta Carrots

PREP TIME 5 MINUTES

COOK TIME 20 MINUTES

SERVES 2

Sweet, savoury and perfectly caramelized – these are such a good way to dress up a simple carrot. The air fryer brings out their natural sweetness, the feta adds a salty kick, and the dill gives everything a fresh lift. A brilliant summer side dish, but I'd happily eat it all year round!

5 medium-sized carrots
1 tbsp sunflower oil, or similar
1 tbsp honey, plus extra to drizzle
1 tsp dried thyme
½ block feta, crumbled
Fresh dill, to garnish
Salt and pepper

1. Peel the carrots, then top, tail and slice them into 2 cm / ¾ inch diagonal pieces. Toss in a bowl with the oil, honey, thyme, and a good pinch of salt and pepper.

2. Tip into the air fryer drawer and cook at 200°C for 20 minutes, giving them a shake a couple of times throughout.

3. Once golden and tender, transfer to a serving bowl. Drizzle with a little extra honey, scatter over a handful of crumbled feta, and finish with fresh dill.

TIP

You can swap the carrots for butternut squash; just cut them into similar-sized chunks and adjust the cook time slightly if needed. The honey-and-feta combo works beautifully with both options.

Perfect Peppers

 PREP TIME 5 MINUTES

 COOK TIME 25 MINUTES

 SERVES – FLEXIBLE, BATCH-COOK AS MUCH AS YOU NEED

Peppers – red, yellow, orange, however many you like, whatever you've got!
Sunflower oil spray, or similar
Salt and pepper

Air frying peppers brings out their natural sweetness and gives them that lovely blistered skin without any faff. I usually make a batch using whatever colours I've got – they're great stirred through pasta, added to salads or just eaten straight from the tray.

ON THE SDIE

1. Slice the peppers in half and remove the stalks and seeds.

2. Place them cut side down in your air fryer drawer. Spray lightly with oil and season with salt and pepper.

3. Air fry at 180°C for 25 minutes – no need to turn!

4. Let them cool slightly, then peel off the skins (they'll lift right off).

5. Slice and serve over salads, stir through pasta, or fold into your favourite dishes for one of your five-a-day!

TIP

The peppers will keep in the fridge in an airtight container for up to four days, so they're ideal for batch-cooking. Try folding them into wraps, tossing into grain bowls or layering into sandwiches for easy flavour. They're also brilliant on a mezze platter with hummus and flatbread.

Yorkshire Puddings

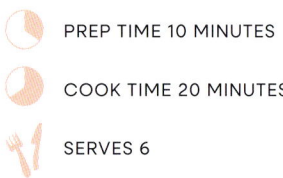

PREP TIME 10 MINUTES

COOK TIME 20 MINUTES

SERVES 6

The air fryer is brilliant for making fresh Yorkshire puds with minimal fuss. Perfect for roast dinners or even as a little treat with gravy on the side. You can easily scale the quantities up or down depending on how many you're making – just make sure you've got enough heat in the tins and resist the urge to peek while they're cooking. Trust the process!

70 g / 2½ oz plain flour
2 medium eggs
100 ml / 3½ fl oz milk
Vegetable or sunflower oil

1. Place the flour in a large bowl, add the eggs and whisk until you have a smooth consistency.

2. Gradually whisk in the milk until fully combined, then set to one side.

3. Add six individual Yorkshire pudding tins (the ones you use in an oven are fine) into your air fryer with a drop of oil in each one (just over a teaspoon in each). Heat on 220°C for 5 minutes (depending on the size of your air fryer, you may need to cook them in two batches).

4. Once the 5 minutes are up, remove the drawers from the air fryer and quickly (but carefully) split the pudding mix evenly between the six tins.

5. Put straight back in the air fryer and air fry for 15 minutes at 190°C – do not open the drawer during this time as they won't rise.

TIP

Make sure your oil is properly hot before adding the batter – it should sizzle as the batter hits it. That's the key to getting that lovely puff and golden crunch. If in doubt, give it an extra minute before pouring the batter in.

ON THE SDIE

Hasselback Baby Potatoes with Crispy Pancetta & Garlic

 PREP TIME 10 MINUTES

 COOK TIME 26 MINUTES

 SERVES 2–3

These take a bit of prep, but they are so worth it! The thin slices help the edges go all crispy while the centres stay soft and fluffy. Add pancetta, garlic and herbs and you've got the perfect combo of salty, crispy and comforting. Delicious served with meat or fish, or just on their own with a dollop of something creamy, such as sour cream and chive dip.

500 g / 1 lb baby potatoes
Oil spray
2 tsp dried parsley
1 tsp lazy garlic (pre-chopped or puréed)
75 g / 2½ oz diced smoked pancetta
Salt and pepper

1. Place each potato into the curved part of a wooden spoon – this helps hold it steady and stops you cutting all the way through. Use a sharp knife to slice thin slits across the top of each potato, about 3 mm / ⅛ inch apart. Repeat with all the potatoes.

2. Add the sliced potatoes to a mixing bowl, spray generously with oil, and mix in the parsley, garlic, salt and black pepper. Toss to coat everything evenly.

3. Transfer the potatoes to the air fryer drawer and air fry at 180°C for 20 minutes, giving them a shake halfway through.

4. After 20 minutes, scatter over the pancetta and return to the air fryer for another 6 minutes at 180°C, until the pancetta is crisp and the potatoes are golden on top.

TIP

Veggie option: Swap the pancetta for crumbled feta once cooked for a veggie-friendly twist.

You can also try switching up the flavour – rosemary and sea salt work well.

Bang Bang Cauliflower with Lime Yoghurt Sauce

 PREP TIME 5 MINUTES

 COOK TIME 15 MINUTES

 SERVES 2–3 (AS A SIDE OR STARTER)

This is my fuss-free, air fryer take on bang bang cauliflower – no batter, no deep-frying, just bold flavours and a fiery kick. The cauliflower turns golden and crispy in the air fryer, then gets coated in a sticky firecracker sauce and served with a cooling lime yoghurt dip on the side. It's a real crowd-pleaser that works brilliantly as a starter or side.

2 tbsp oil
½ tsp garlic granules
2 tsp smoked paprika
1 large cauliflower (approx. 500 g / 1 lb), cut into florets
120 g / 4 oz sachet firecracker stir-fry sauce
Salt and pepper

FOR THE LIME YOGHURT SAUCE
3 tbsp Greek yoghurt
Zest of ½ lime
Juice of ½ lime
Black pepper

TO SERVE
Chopped spring onions
Sesame seeds
Fresh coriander (optional)

1. Add the oil, garlic granules, smoked paprika, salt and pepper to a large bowl and mix. Add the cauliflower florets and toss until evenly coated.

2. Place the cauliflower in the air fryer drawer in an even layer. Air fry at 190°C for 12 minutes, shaking halfway through.

3. Meanwhile, make the lime yoghurt sauce: mix the yoghurt, lime zest and juice and a crack of black pepper in a small bowl until smooth.

4. Once the cauliflower is cooked, tip it out of the air fryer, remove the crisper tray with silicone tongs, then return the cauliflower to the drawer. Stir through the firecracker sauce and air fry for a further 3 minutes at 190°C, until heated through and slightly caramelized.

5. Serve hot, scattered with spring onions, sesame seeds and coriander, with the lime yoghurt sauce on the side for dipping.

ON THE SDIE

TIP

This one's got a proper punch of heat – if you're not big on spice, swap the firecracker sauce for a mild stir-fry sauce, such as sweet teriyaki or hoisin. Still full of flavour, just less of a firework!

Harissa-roasted Courgettes with Feta & Mint

 PREP TIME 5 MINUTES

 COOK TIME 15 MINUTES

 SERVES 2

This is one of those sides that takes barely any effort but tastes like something you'd get at a restaurant. The courgettes go beautifully soft with a little char at the edges, the harissa brings a warm kick, and the feta and mint give it a lovely fresh finish. Great with grilled chicken or lamb, or served cold as part of a mezze spread.

2 courgettes (approx. 170 g / 6 oz each)
3 tsp harissa paste (2 tsp for the courgettes, 1 tsp for the yoghurt sauce)
½ tsp dried oregano
Oil spray
Squeeze of lemon juice
30 g / 1 oz feta, crumbled
1 tbsp chopped mint
2 tsp Greek yoghurt
Salt and pepper

TO SERVE
Lemon wedges

1. Top and tail the courgettes, then slice in half lengthways and cut into 1 cm / ½ inch half-moons.

2. In a bowl, toss the courgette slices with 2 teaspoons of the harissa paste, the oregano, a couple of sprays of oil, salt and pepper. Stir until evenly coated.

3. Tip into the air fryer and cook at 190°C for 15 minutes, shaking halfway through, until golden and just crisp at the edges.

4. Transfer to a serving dish, squeeze over the lemon juice, scatter with feta and finish with the chopped mint.

5. Mix the yoghurt with the remaining harissa paste and serve on the side or dolloped over the courgettes, with a couple of lemon wedges.

TIP

Not a fan of harissa? Switch it for pesto for a totally different twist. It also works a treat stirred through couscous or bulgur wheat to make it more of a meal.

Simple Sautéed Potatoes

PREP TIME 10 MINUTES

COOK TIME 20 MINUTES

SERVES 2–3

These air-fried sautéed potatoes are golden, crispy and completely addictive. Perfect as a side dish, or even as a snack with dips, they're quick to prep and endlessly versatile – just switch up the seasoning to suit your mood.

500 g potatoes, thinly sliced
Oil spray
1–2 tsp peri peri seasoning (or your favourite spice blend)
Salt and pepper

TO SERVE
Garlic mayo (optional – use a vegan mayo to keep it plant-based)

1. Slice the potatoes thinly, then rinse in cold water to remove excess starch. Pat dry thoroughly with a clean cloth or kitchen roll.

2. Place the potatoes in a large bowl, spray with oil, season with peri peri and a little salt and pepper, then toss to coat.

3. Transfer to the air fryer drawer in an even layer. Air fry at 200°C for 20 minutes, shaking a couple of times throughout. Spray with a little extra oil if they look like they need it.

4. Serve hot, with a good dollop of garlic mayo or your favourite sauce for dipping.

TIP

Rinsing and drying the potatoes really well is the key to crispiness. peri peri is one of my favourite flavours, but you can use paprika, garlic salt or even curry powder for a tasty twist.

Loaded Cheeseburger Fries

 PREP TIME 10 MINUTES

 COOK TIME 23–28 MINUTES

 SERVES 3–4 (SHARING)

All the best bits of a cheeseburger, but in snack form! I first spotted a cheeseburger nachos dish in Tesco, but I think this dirty-fries version is even better – more substantial, messier and seriously satisfying. Perfect for sharing ... or not!

300 g / 10½ oz beef mince
½ onion, diced
1 tsp smoked paprika
½ tsp mild chilli powder (or more if you like it spicy)
700 g / 1½ lb frozen skinny fries
100 g / 3½ oz mature Cheddar cheese, grated
Salt and pepper

FOR THE BURGER SAUCE
2 tbsp mayonnaise
1 tbsp ketchup
1 tbsp American mustard
5 sliced gherkins, finely chopped

TO SERVE
1 large tomato, diced
Extra onion, diced (optional)

1. Mix together the beef mince and onion and place in a lined air fryer drawer. Cook at 200°C for 7 minutes.

2. Add the paprika, chilli powder, salt and pepper, stir through, and air fry for another 2 minutes at 200°C. Tip the mince into a bowl and set aside.

3. Air fry the skinny fries as per the packet instructions – this is normally 10 minutes from fresh or 15 minutes from frozen at 200°C – making sure to shake them a couple of times throughout to get a crispy end result. Once cooked, tip them into a bowl, add a liner to your air fryer drawer (for easier serving), then return the fries to the drawer.

4. Top the fries in the drawer with the cooked mince and scatter with grated Cheddar. Air fry at 180°C for 4 minutes until the cheese is melted and gooey.

5. Meanwhile, mix together the mayonnaise, ketchup, mustard and chopped gherkins to make the burger sauce.

6. Lift the loaded fries out using the liner, transfer to a serving dish, then finish with diced tomato, extra onion (if using), and a generous dollop of the burger sauce dotted throughout.

TIP

If you've got a two-drawer air fryer, cook the mince and fries at the same time. With a single drawer, do the mince first, then the fries, and then combine it all as per the instructions.

Tenderstem Broccoli with Sesame, Honey & Lime

 PREP TIME 5 MINUTES

 COOK TIME 8–10 MINUTES

 SERVES 2

Crunchy, nutty and just the right amount of char – this is one of those sides you'll want to eat straight from the tray! The drizzle of honey at the end balances the savoury flavours, while lime keeps it fresh and zesty. It's delicious as a side, but you can also toss it through rice or noodles to turn it into a light meal.

200 g / 7 oz tenderstem broccoli
2 tsp sesame oil
2 tsp soy sauce
½ tsp garlic granules
1 tsp sesame seeds
Salt and pepper

TO SERVE
Drizzle of honey (approx. 1 tsp)
Juice of ½ lime
Dash of soy (approx. ½ tsp)
Extra sesame seeds
Fresh red chilli, finely sliced (optional)

1. Toss the broccoli with sesame oil, soy sauce, garlic granules, sesame seeds, and a pinch of salt and pepper.

2. Place in the air fryer drawer and cook at 190°C for 8–10 minutes, shaking halfway through, until slightly charred but still with a bit of bite.

3. Drizzle with honey, squeeze over the lime juice, and finish with a dash more soy. Scatter with extra sesame seeds and fresh chilli if you like, toss to coat and serve immediately.

TIP

Don't overcrowd the air fryer drawer – giving the broccoli space helps it char instead of steam. A scatter of crushed peanuts or cashews on top is a lovely extra crunch, and it's especially good served with simple air fryer salmon.

Sweet Treats

Apple, Cinnamon & Pecan Flapjacks

- PREP TIME 5 MINUTES
- COOK TIME 29 MINUTES
- SERVES 8

I first made these when I had a lonely apple in the fruit bowl and fancied a twist on my usual flapjacks. They're simple, comforting and smell incredible as they cook. Soft and chewy in the centre, crispy at the edges, with a lovely crunch from the nuts – these flapjacks are full of cosy autumn flavours. The grated apple keeps them beautifully moist, while the cinnamon and pecans add warmth and texture. Perfect for lunchboxes or an afternoon treat with a cuppa.

110 g / 3¾ oz unsalted butter, diced
2 tbsp golden syrup
90 g / 3 oz light brown sugar
250 g / 8½ oz porridge oats
1 tsp vanilla extract
1 tsp ground cinnamon
1 medium eating apple, coarsely grated (excess juice squeezed out)
50 g / 1¾ oz chopped pecans or walnuts

1. Add the butter, golden syrup and brown sugar to an air fryer-friendly dish. Air fry for 4 minutes at 180°C until melted, then stir until smooth.

2. Transfer to a bowl and stir in the oats, vanilla extract, cinnamon, grated apple and nuts until everything is well coated.

3. Divide the mixture between eight silicone moulds, or press into one large silicone or foil tray.

4. Air fry at 150°C for 25 minutes, until golden and set around the edges.

5. Leave to cool in the moulds for 10 minutes before removing (they'll firm up as they cool). Make a cuppa and enjoy that perfect apple-cinnamon smell wafting through the kitchen!

TIP

Be sure to squeeze out as much juice from the grated apple as possible so the flapjacks don't end up too wet. Don't waste the juice, though – pour it into a glass and enjoy a sweet shot of fresh apple juice while you cook!

Double Chocolate Brioche Pudding Cups

 PREP TIME 10 MINUTES

 COOK TIME 13 MINUTES

 SERVES 2 AS LARGE PORTIONS (OR AS 4 SMALLER PORTIONS)

Sometimes you just need something chocolatey and warm, fast! I first spotted a brioche pudding idea in one of Hayley Dean's cookbooks and loved the simplicity. Over time, I've adapted it into a version that's become a go-to on a Sunday afternoon, using soft brioche rolls (as I always seem to have some in the cupboard!) and a touch of cinnamon for a cosy twist. These little puddings are rich, gooey and ridiculously easy to throw together. The buttery brioche soaks up the chocolate custard to make something halfway between a brownie and a bread pudding – perfect for an after-dinner treat. These are best eaten warm with a scoop of ice cream or a dollop of custard.

25 g / ¾ oz unsalted butter, melted and cooled (melt 1 minute in the microwave)
1½ tbsp light brown soft sugar
1 tbsp cocoa powder
½ tsp cinnamon
100 ml / 3½ fl oz single cream
1 large egg
1 tsp vanilla extract
50 g / 1¾ oz chocolate chips or chunks (dark, milk or a mix)
4 mini butter brioche rolls (the kind you get in a pack of 8)

TO SERVE
Vanilla ice cream, cream or custard

1. In a bowl, whisk together the cooled butter, brown sugar, cocoa powder, cinnamon, cream, egg and vanilla extract until smooth. Stir through the chocolate chips.

2. Tear or cut the brioche rolls into bite-sized chunks and tip into the chocolate mixture, then stir everything together and leave for 5 minutes for the bread to soak up the mixture.

3. Divide the mixture between two silicone/air fryer-friendly dishes.

4. Air fry at 160°C for 13 minutes, until puffed and just set in the middle. The tops should look glossy and slightly crisp. (You'll be able to smell it once it's done – it smells so good!)

5. Serve warm with a scoop of ice cream or cream (you'll probably have some left over from the mixture) or a dollop of custard.

TIP

Don't skip letting the butter cool – if it's too hot when you mix it in, you'll risk scrambling the egg. No one wants scrambled egg pudding!

Cinnamon Nachos with Chocolate Dip

 PREP TIME 5 MINUTES

 COOK TIME 7 MINUTES

 SERVES 2

These are seriously good – sweet, crunchy, and perfect for dunking into a pool of melty chocolate. It's the kind of recipe that feels like a proper treat, but only takes minutes to pull together. Great for sharing ... although you might not want to!

110 g / 3¾ oz milk chocolate (in its plastic wrapper)
2 large tortilla wraps
50 g / 1¾ oz unsalted butter, melted
1 tsp cinnamon
2 tsp caster sugar

1. Place the bar of milk chocolate (still in its plastic wrapper) into a shallow bowl and cover with boiling water. Set aside to melt while you make the nachos.

2. Cut the wraps into triangles and place in a large Tupperware container with a lid.

3. In a small bowl, mix the melted butter with the cinnamon and sugar.

4. Pour the butter mixture over the wrap pieces. Put the lid on and shake until the wraps are evenly coated.

5. Transfer the wraps to the air fryer drawer in an even layer. Place a rack over the top to stop them flying around once they start to crisp (if you don't have one, just keep an eye on them).

6. Air fry at 190°C for 7 minutes, until golden and crunchy.

7. Tip the nachos onto a serving dish. Snip the corner of the chocolate wrapper and squeeze the melted chocolate into a small bowl for dipping.

TIP

Milk chocolate works perfectly here, but you can switch it up with whatever chocolate bar you like – just make sure it's sealed in plastic, not foil, so it melts safely in hot water.

Super-easy S'mores

 PREP TIME 4 MINUTES

 COOK TIME 6 MINUTES

 SERVES 4–6

A similar recipe went viral online, and once I saw it I just had to give it a go! It's ridiculously simple but such a crowd-pleaser. You just chuck everything in and 6 minutes later you've got golden marshmallows, melty chocolate and biscuits ready for dipping. Naughty, yes, but so worth it!

1 bag giant marshmallows (approx. 15 marshmallows)
100 g / 3½ oz chocolate buttons
1 packet (360 g / 12½ oz) digestive biscuits

1. Line your air fryer drawer with a paper liner that has sides (and no holes). Tightly pack the marshmallows in a single even layer inside.

2. Air fry at 180°C for 4 minutes, until the marshmallows are puffed and golden.

3. Push the chocolate buttons between the marshmallows, then return to the air fryer for 2 minutes at 180°C, until the chocolate is just melted.

4. Carefully lift the paper liner out of the drawer and transfer the s'mores to a serving dish. Scoop up the gooey marshmallow and chocolate with digestive biscuits and dig in!

TIP

If you're more into savoury than sweet, check out my Brie & Chorizo S'mores (page 62) – just as melty but with a savoury cheesy twist. Both are worth making – maybe not on the same day, though, as that would be crazy on the calorie front!

SWEET TREATS

Caramelized Pineapple Pastries

PREP TIME 5 MINUTES

COOK TIME 16 MINUTES

SERVES 4

These are golden, sticky and properly delicious – like an air fryer version of an upside-down tart! You get juicy caramelized pineapple, crisp puff pastry, a hit of cinnamon and a drizzle of honey to finish. They look impressive but are ridiculously easy to make. Great as a dessert, afternoon snack, or even for a cheeky brunch treat.

1 tbsp caster sugar
½ tsp ground cinnamon
4 pineapple rings from a can, cut in half
4 × 15 cm / 6 inch squares of ready-rolled puff pastry
1 egg, beaten (for egg wash)
Honey, to drizzle

TO SERVE
Crème fraîche or vanilla ice cream (optional)

1. Line your air fryer basket or drawer with baking parchment.

2. Mix the caster sugar and cinnamon together, then sprinkle a little over the parchment.

3. Place two pineapple halves side by side on the sugar, slightly overlapping. Repeat with the remaining pineapple to make four portions, sprinkling each with a little more cinnamon sugar.

4. Lay a square of puff pastry over each portion, poke a small hole in the centre to let steam escape, then brush with egg wash.

5. Air fry at 180°C for 16 minutes, until the pastry is puffed and golden. If you have a two-drawer air fryer, you can cook two pastries in each drawer. With a single drawer, you may be able to fit all four at once, but if not, just cook in batches – they only take 16 minutes, so you won't be waiting long.

6. Carefully lift the pastries out onto a plate or board. Flip them over, peel away the parchment, place on a serving dish and drizzle with honey.

7. Serve warm with crème fraîche or ice cream as you prefer.

TIP

You can switch out the pineapple for other tinned or soft fruits like peaches, pears or plums. Just make sure they're not too wet before adding them – pat dry with kitchen roll to help the pastry crisp up.

Apple & Cinnamon Pies

PREP TIME 10 MINUTES

COOK TIME 16 MINUTES

SERVES 5

These little pies are so simple but always feel like a treat. Buttery puff pastry, sweet apple and a hint of cinnamon – you just can't go wrong. I love them warm from the air fryer with custard or ice cream, but they're just as good cold the next day with a cuppa.

320 g / 11 oz sheet ready-rolled puff pastry
1 tin Princes apple filling
Ground cinnamon
1 medium egg, beaten (for egg wash)
3 tsp demerara sugar

TO SERVE
Custard or ice cream (optional)

1. Lay out the pastry sheet and cut it in half lengthways, then into five even sections widthways to give ten equal rectangles.

2. Spoon some apple filling into the centre of five of the pastry rectangles, leaving a 1 cm / ½ inch border around the edges.

3. Sprinkle a little cinnamon over the apple filling, then brush the pastry borders with egg wash.

4. Top each with the remaining five pastry rectangles and press the edges with the back of a fork to seal.

5. Cut three small slits diagonally across the top of each pie.

6. If you have a paper liner, place it in your air fryer drawer (this makes removing the pies easier, but it's optional). Arrange the pies in a single layer.

7. Brush the tops with more egg wash and sprinkle with demerara sugar.

8. Air fry at 180°C for 16 minutes, until puffed and golden.

9. Serve warm with custard or ice cream as you prefer.

TIP

These also work really well with Princes red or black cherry fillings – just skip the cinnamon and keep everything else the same.

Peaches & Cream Pastry Puffs

 PREP TIME 10 MINUTES

 COOK TIME 10 MINUTES

 SERVES 12–18 (DEPENDING ON PASTRY-CUTTER SIZE)

Golden, flaky pastry filled with whipped cream and juicy peaches – this is such a simple but elegant dessert. Using tinned peaches keeps it fuss-free, but you still get all the flavour and freshness. It looks like you've gone to loads of effort, but it's actually really simple ... the cream is the most complicated bit, and even that's easy with an electric hand whisk.

1 320 g / 11 oz sheet ready-rolled puff pastry
1 egg, beaten (for egg wash)
Granulated sugar, for sprinkling
30 g / 1 oz icing sugar, plus extra for dusting
250 ml / 8½ fl oz double cream
200 g / 7 oz tinned peach slices, drained and patted dry

1. Lay out the puff pastry sheet and cut out shapes with a cutter of your choice – hearts, circles, whatever you fancy (even simple squares work well and look great, plus there's no waste from the pastry).

2. Transfer the cut-outs to your air fryer drawer. Brush with egg wash and sprinkle with granulated sugar.

3. Air fry at 170°C for 10 minutes until golden and puffed. Allow to cool completely.

4. Meanwhile, whip the icing sugar and double cream together until thick and pipeable.

5. Carefully slice each pastry in half. Add a swirl of cream to the bottom half, then top with slices of peach. Pop the pastry lid back on and dust with icing sugar.

6. Serve straight away and enjoy!

TIP

Make sure the pastry is completely cooled before adding the cream, otherwise it will melt. Swap the peaches for other fruits like mango or raspberries, or replace the whipped cream with clotted cream if you're looking to save time.

Honey & Cinnamon Baked Pears

 PREP TIME 5 MINUTES

 COOK TIME 15–20 MINUTES

 SERVES 2

These feel indulgent but are actually a lighter pudding option, especially if you serve them with a dollop of Greek yoghurt instead of ice cream. Warm, soft pears with honey and cinnamon – simple but so satisfying, and a great way of getting one of your five-a-day!

2 Conference pears (approx. 220 g / 7½ oz each)
Ground cinnamon
Honey, for drizzling

TO SERVE
Greek yoghurt and chopped nuts or ice cream (optional)

1. Core the pears and slice them in half from top to bottom.

2. Place a paper liner (without holes) in your air fryer drawer, or use an air fryer-friendly dish if you don't have liners – this will stop the honey from dripping through. Arrange the pears flesh side up, side by side.

3. Sprinkle generously with cinnamon and drizzle with honey.

4. Air fry at 170°C for 15 minutes. After 10 minutes, open the drawer and brush the pears with any honey that has collected at the bottom.

5. Check the pears are soft by inserting a sharp knife – if they're still firm, cook for a further 5 minutes.

6. Serve warm with a dollop of Greek yoghurt and chopped nuts, or go indulgent with a scoop of ice cream.

SWEET TREATS

TIP

Swap the pears for apples if that's what you've got in the fruit bowl – they work just as well. These also work really well chopped up and served with my Super-nutty Cinnamon Granola (see page 30) – perfect for breakfast or a more wholesome dessert.

Gooey Chocolate Orange Brownies

PREP TIME 15 MINUTES

COOK TIME 30 MINUTES

SERVES 6–8

Rich, fudgy, and full of chocolate-orange flavour, these brownies are baked to stay soft and gooey in the middle. Think of them like a melt-in-the-middle cake with that classic brownie taste – perfect served warm with a scoop of ice cream for an indulgent pudding.

120 g / 4 oz chocolate orange (90 g / 3 oz melted, 30 g / 1 oz chopped)
80 g / 2¾ oz unsalted butter
175 g / 6 oz light brown sugar
2 large eggs, beaten
1 tsp orange essence
Zest of 1 orange (optional, for extra flavour)
60 g / 2 oz self-raising flour
30 g / 1 oz cocoa powder

TO SERVE
Ice cream or cream

1. For a two-drawer air fryer, you can cook directly in the drawer – just remove the crisper tray, spray lightly with oil and line with parchment. Alternatively, line a baking tin that fits inside your air fryer with parchment paper and set aside.

2. Break 90 g / 3 oz of the chocolate into a saucepan with the butter, and gently melt over a low heat. Set aside to cool slightly.

3. In a mixing bowl, whisk the sugar and eggs together until pale and creamy. Stir in the orange essence (and zest, if using).

4. Pour in the cooled chocolate and butter mixture, then whisk until smooth.

5. Sift the flour and cocoa powder together, then fold into the mixture until just combined.

6. Roughly chop the remaining 30 g / 1 oz of chocolate and fold it through the batter. Pour everything into the lined tin or drawer and smooth the top.

7. Air fry at 180°C for 30 minutes. The top should be set but the centre will still be gooey.

8. Leave to cool slightly, then serve warm with ice cream or cream for a rich, pudding-style brownie.

TIP

If you prefer a more traditional set, bake at 170°C for 35–45 minutes instead. Or, divide the mixture between eight silicone cupcake moulds and air fry at 170°C for 16–18 minutes for a super-speedy bake. For an extra twist, sprinkle a tiny bit of sea salt on top before baking to balance the sweetness.

Sticky Toffee Ginger Pudding

PREP TIME 15 MINUTES

COOK TIME 25 MINUTES

SERVES 4

Inspired by Mary Berry's classic Sticky Toffee Pudding recipe, this is my air fryer take on it! It's rich, sumptuous and full of flavour, with an added hint of ground ginger for warmth and spice. A perfect recipe to knock up to finish off a Sunday-roast kind of day.

75 g / 2½ oz unsalted butter, softened
130 g / 4½ oz light brown soft sugar
1½ tbsp golden syrup
1½ tbsp treacle
2 small eggs
130 g / 4½ oz self-raising flour
¾ tsp baking powder
¾ tsp ground ginger
1½ tbsp milk

FOR THE TOFFEE SAUCE
75 g / 2½ oz light brown sugar
40 g / 1½ oz unsalted butter
120 ml / 4 fl oz double cream

TO SERVE
Ice cream or cream (optional)

1. Lightly spray or grease four individual silicone moulds that fit inside your air fryer drawer.

2. Cream together the butter and sugar until pale and fluffy. Beat in the golden syrup, treacle and eggs.

3. Sift in the flour, baking powder and ginger. Fold together gently, then stir in the milk to loosen.

4. Divide the mixture evenly between the moulds. Place in the air fryer basket or drawer and cook at 165°C for 25 minutes, until risen and springy to the touch.

5. Meanwhile, make the sauce: heat the sugar and butter together in a saucepan and stir until smooth, then slowly add in the cream, stirring slowly until smooth and slightly thickened.

6. Turn the puddings out of the moulds, pour over the warm toffee sauce, and enjoy with ice cream or cream if you like. Yum!

TIP

If you don't have individual moulds, you can use one medium-sized air fryer-friendly dish and slice it up to serve. This will increase the cooking time slightly – just add a few extra minutes and check it's cooked through with a skewer (it should come out clean when it's ready).

Banana & Chocolate Chip Cakes

 PREP TIME 10 MINUTES

 COOK TIME 15 MINUTES

 SERVES 8

There always seems to be that one banana getting a bit too soft in the fruit bowl – and this is the best way to put it to good use! These little cakes are light, fluffy and packed with chocolate chips. They're quick to make, perfect with a cuppa, and a great little bake for the air fryer.

75 g / 2½ oz plain flour
75 g / 2½ oz caster sugar
½ tsp bicarbonate of soda
½ tsp baking powder
1 medium egg
1 tbsp milk
50 g / 1¾ oz unsalted butter, melted and cooled
1 ripe banana, mashed
50 g / 1¾ oz milk chocolate chips

TO SERVE
Icing sugar, for dusting (optional)

1. In a large bowl, mix together the flour, sugar, bicarbonate of soda and baking powder.

2. Add the egg, milk, cooled butter and mashed banana. Stir until everything is combined.

3. Fold in the chocolate chips until evenly distributed.

4. Divide the mixture between eight silicone muffin cups and place them in the air fryer drawer.

5. Air fry at 160°C for 15 minutes, until risen and golden. To check they're done, insert a skewer into the centre of a cake – if it comes out clean, they're ready.

6. Dust with icing sugar if you'd like a little extra sweetness, then serve warm or at room temperature.

TIP

Let the melted butter cool before mixing it in, otherwise it can scramble the egg and affect the texture of the cakes.

Mince Pie Bites

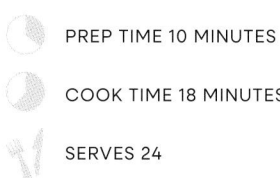

PREP TIME 10 MINUTES

COOK TIME 18 MINUTES

SERVES 24

Sticky, sweet and ridiculously moreish! These are such an easy win when you want a last-minute festive treat – but honestly, I make them well beyond December. They're bite-sized, golden and perfect for sharing. Pictured overleaf.

320 g / 11 oz sheet ready-rolled puff pastry
1 jar rich fruit mincemeat (400 g / 14 oz)
1 small egg, beaten (for egg wash)
Icing sugar, for dusting

1. Lay out the pastry sheet, cut in half widthways, then cut each half into thirds so you have six strips.

2. Cut through the centre lengthways, then each in half again, so you end up with 24 squares of pastry.

3. Place 1 heaped teaspoon of mincemeat in the centre of each square of pastry.

4. On each piece of pastry, pull together all four corners and squeeze in the centre to make a parcel.

5. Transfer the pastries to the air fryer, brush with egg wash, and air fry for 18 minutes at 180°C.

6. Leave to cool for 5 minutes in the air fryer (the mincemeat gets VERY hot), then transfer to a serving platter and use a sieve to dust with the icing sugar.

TIP

You can easily switch up the flavours – try a spoonful of jam, lemon curd, Nutella or even peanut butter and chocolate chips for an all-year-round sweet fix.

Index

apples: apple & cinnamon pies 174
  apple, cinnamon & pecan flapjacks 166
asparagus: prosciutto-wrapped fish with pesto & asparagus 105
  salmon & asparagus with curried potatoes & chickpeas 106
aubergines: roasted aubergine with herby couscous & harissa yoghurt 137

bacon: devils on horseback 70
  fluffy French toast with bacon & blueberries 14
  roasted tomato, bacon & basil soup 53
bagels: the ultimate tuna bagel melt 40
banana & chocolate chip cakes 184
bang bang cauliflower 157
bao buns, peanut satay veg 138
beans: creamy garlic butter beans on toast with chorizo 48
  crunchy Marmite butter beans 61
  feta, beans & egg bowl 24
  smoky shakshuka with butter beans 23
beef: burger tacos 100
  loaded cheeseburger fries 161
berry compote, mixed 29
blueberries, fluffy French toast with bacon & 14
Boursin & tomato pasta 128
bread: cheesy garlic bread bites 72
  creamy garlic butter beans on toast 48
  creamy garlic mushrooms & crispy pancetta on sourdough 20
  crostini with roasted tomatoes & goat's cheese 78
  garlic & herb croutons 45
  see also brioche; pitta breads
brioche: breakfast brioche with mushrooms, chorizo & poached eggs 26
  double chocolate brioche pudding cups 168
  fluffy French toast 14
broccoli: broccoli stalk burgers 135
  Tenderstem broccoli with sesame, honey & lime 162

brownies, gooey chocolate orange 180
burgers: broccoli stalk burgers 135
  burger tacos 100
  crispy fish burgers 116
  halloumi burger 131
  Thai turkey burgers 102
burrata salad, the best ever 38

cabbage: slaws 56, 102
cakes: banana & chocolate chip cakes 184
  gooey chocolate orange brownies 180
carrots: carrot & parsnip peel crisps 76
  honey & feta carrots 148
cauliflower: bang bang cauliflower 157
  cheesy cauliflower steaks 123
cheese: 7-minute pesto pitta pizzas 44
  baked feta with nduja & roasted peppers 54
  baked sweet potato with goat's cheese & sun-dried tomatoes 132
  the best ever burrata salad 38
  Boursin & tomato pasta 128
  Brie & chorizo savoury s'mores 62
  broccoli stalk burgers 135
  burger tacos 100
  Camembert three ways 80–1
  caramelized onion & goat's cheese tarts 64
  cheesy cauliflower steaks 123
  cheesy garlic bread bites 72
  chicken Parmesan schnitzel 98
  chicken, pesto, sun-dried tomato & Parmesan wrap 50
  crostini with roasted tomatoes & goat's cheese 78
  easy-peasy cheese & chive scones 59
  egg Marmite & cheesy crumpets 18
  feta, beans & egg bowl 24
  halloumi burger 131
  harissa-roasted courgettes with feta & mint 158
  honey & feta carrots 148
  loaded cheeseburger fries 161
  Marmite macaroni cheese 97
  pesto Parmesan mushroom pasta 126
  pigs in blankets, Brie & cranberry sausage rolls 75
  quick & easy egg cups 25
  red pesto & cheese bites 69

  spanakopita bites 66
  spinach, sun-dried tomato & goat's cheese frittata 34
  truffle Parmesan fries 144
  tuna & cheese loaded potato skins 115
  the ultimate tuna bagel melt 40
chicken: the best ever Coronation chicken 84
  chicken Parmesan schnitzel 98
  chicken, pesto, sun-dried tomato & Parmesan wrap 50
  chicken shawarma pitta pockets 47
  homemade chicken nuggets 86
  quick southern-fried chicken thighs 88
chickpeas, salmon & asparagus with curried potatoes & 106
chillies: sweet chilli & lime mayo 108
chips, sweet & savoury pitta 77
chocolate: banana & chocolate chip cakes 184
  cinnamon nachos with chocolate dip 170
  double chocolate brioche pudding cups 168
  gooey chocolate orange brownies 180
  super-easy s'mores 171
chorizo: breakfast brioche with mushrooms, chorizo & poached eggs 26
  Brie & chorizo savoury s'mores 62
  creamy Camembert with spicy chorizo 80
  creamy garlic butter beans on toast with chorizo 48
cinnamon: apple & cinnamon pies 174
  apple, cinnamon & pecan flapjacks 166
  cinnamon nachos 170
  honey & cinnamon baked pears 179
  sweet pitta chips 77
compote, mixed berry 29
Coronation chicken, the best ever 84
courgettes, harissa-roasted 158
couscous: roasted aubergine with herby couscous & harissa yoghurt 137
cranberry sauce: pigs in blankets, Brie & cranberry sausage rolls 75
cream: peaches & cream pastry puffs 176

188

crisps: carrot & parsnip peel
   crisps 76
   kale crisps 65
crostini with roasted tomatoes
   & goat's cheese 78
croutons, garlic & herb 45
crumpets, egg Marmite &
   cheesy 18
curry powder: the best ever
   Coronation chicken 84
   crispy tandoori baby
      potatoes 142
   salmon & asparagus with curried
      potatoes & chickpeas 106

devils on horseback 70
Digestive biscuits: super-easy
   s'mores 171

eggs: breakfast brioche with
   mushrooms, chorizo & poached
   eggs 26
   easy egg taco boats 17
   egg Marmite & cheesy
      crumpets 18
   feta, beans & egg bowl 24
   harissa poached eggs 33
   poached eggs 28
   quick & easy egg cups 25
   Scotch eggs 42
   smoky shakshuka 23
   soft- and hard-boiled eggs 28
   spinach, sun-dried tomato &
      goat's cheese frittata 34

filo pastry: spanakopita bites 66
fish: crispy fish burgers 116
   miso-glazed fish with sticky rice
      & greens 118
   prosciutto-wrapped fish with
      pesto & asparagus 105
   salmon & asparagus with curried
      potatoes & chickpeas 106
   salmon en croute 122
   salmon fish finger wraps 56
   sticky teriyaki salmon
      traybake 111
   tuna & cheese loaded potato
      skins 115
   the ultimate tuna bagel melt 40
flapjacks, apple, cinnamon &
   pecan 166
French toast, fluffy 14
fries: loaded cheeseburger
   fries 161
   truffle Parmesan fries 144
frittata, spinach, sun-dried tomato
   & goat's cheese 34

garlic: cheesy garlic bread bites 72
   creamy garlic butter beans on
      toast with chorizo 48
   creamy garlic mushrooms &
      crispy pancetta on
      sourdough 20
   garlic & herb chips 77
   garlic & herb croutons 45
   garlic peri peri wedges 146
   hasselback baby potatoes with
      crispy pancetta & garlic 154
   honey & garlic Camembert 81
   lemon garlic butter prawns with
      linguine 121
ginger: sticky toffee ginger
   pudding 183
gnocchi with mushrooms, spinach,
   ricotta, walnuts & lemon 134
granola, super-nutty cinnamon 30
greens, miso-glazed fish with
   sticky rice & 118

halloumi burger 131
harissa: harissa poached eggs 33
   harissa-roasted courgettes 158
   harissa yoghurt 137
hasselback baby potatoes 154
herbs: garlic & herb chips 77
   garlic & herb croutons 45
   roasted aubergine with herby
      couscous & harissa yoghurt 137
honey: honey & cinnamon baked
   pears 179
   honey & feta carrots 148
   honey & garlic Camembert 81
   honey & mustard pork chops 90
   Tenderstem broccoli with
      sesame, honey & lime 162

kale crisps 65
koftas, super simple lamb 101

lamb: lamb chops with minted
   pea mash 94
   super simple lamb koftas 101
lemons: gnocchi with mushrooms,
   spinach, ricotta, walnuts & lemon
   134
   lemon garlic butter prawns with
      linguine 121
   lemon mayo slaw 56
limes: lime yoghurt sauce 157
   sweet chilli & lime mayo 108
   Tenderstem broccoli with
      sesame, honey & lime 162
loaded cheeseburger fries 161

macaroni cheese, Marmite 97

Marmite: crunchy Marmite butter
   beans 61
   egg Marmite & cheesy
      crumpets 18
   Marmite macaroni cheese 97
marshmallows: super-easy
   s'mores 171
mayonnaise: sweet chilli & lime
   mayo 108
   tartare sauce 116
meatball pasta bake, sausage 93
Mexican rice-stuffed peppers 125
mince pie bites 185
miso-glazed fish with sticky rice
   & greens 118
mushrooms: breakfast brioche
   with mushrooms, chorizo &
   poached eggs 26
   creamy garlic mushrooms
      & crispy pancetta on
      sourdough 20
   gnocchi with mushrooms,
      spinach, ricotta, walnuts
      & lemon 134
   pesto Parmesan mushroom
      pasta 126
mustard: honey & mustard pork
   chops 90

nachos, cinnamon 170
nduja: baked feta with nduja
   & roasted peppers 54
nectarines: the best ever burrata
   salad 38
noodles: prawn air fry 112
nuts: super-nutty cinnamon
   granola 30

oats: apple, cinnamon & pecan
   flapjacks 166
   super-nutty cinnamon
      granola 30
onions: caramelized onion & goat's
   cheese tarts 64

pancetta: creamy garlic
   mushrooms & crispy pancetta on
   sourdough 20
   hasselback baby potatoes with
      crispy pancetta 154
Parma ham: the best ever burrata
   salad 38
parsnips: carrot & parsnip peel
   crisps 76
pasta: Boursin & tomato pasta 128
   lemon garlic butter prawns with
      linguine 121
   Marmite macaroni cheese 97

INDEX

189

pesto Parmesan mushroom
   pasta 126
sausage meatball pasta bake 93
pastries: caramelized pineapple
   pastries 173
   peaches & cream pastry
      puffs 176
pea mash, minted 94
peanut satay veg bao buns 138
pears, honey & cinnamon
   baked 179
pecans: apple, cinnamon & pecan
   flapjacks 166
peppers: baked feta with nduja
   & roasted peppers 54
   harissa poached eggs with
      spinach & peppers 33
   Mexican rice-stuffed peppers 125
   perfect peppers 151
peri peri seasoning: garlic peri peri
   wedges 146
pesto: 7-minute pesto pitta
   pizzas 44
   chicken, pesto, sun-dried tomato
      & Parmesan wrap 50
   pesto Parmesan mushroom
      pasta 126
   prosciutto-wrapped fish with
      pesto & asparagus 105
   red pesto & cheese bites 69
pies: apple & cinnamon pies 174
   puff pastry pie top 87
pigs in blankets, Brie & cranberry
   sausage rolls 75
pineapple: caramelized pineapple
   pastries 173
pitta breads: 7-minute pesto pitta
   pizzas 44
   chicken shawarma pitta
      pockets 47
   sweet & savoury pitta chips 77
pizzas, 7-minute pesto pitta 44
pork chops, honey & mustard 90
potatoes: crispy tandoori baby
   potatoes 142
   garlic peri peri wedges 146
   hasselback baby potatoes 154
   salmon & asparagus with curried
      potatoes & chickpeas 106
   simple sautéed potatoes 160
   tuna & cheese loaded potato
      skins 115
prawns: breaded prawn tacos 108
   lemon garlic butter prawns with
      linguine 121
   prawn air fry 112
prosciutto-wrapped fish with
   pesto & asparagus 105
puff pastry: apple & cinnamon

pies 174
Camembert & red onion chutney
   in puff pastry 81
caramelized pineapple pastries
   173
mince pie bites 185
peaches & cream pastry
   puffs 176
pigs in blankets, Brie & cranberry
   sausage rolls 75
puff pastry pie top 87
red pesto & cheese bites 69
salmon en croute 122

red onion chutney: Camembert
   & red onion chutney in puff
   pastry 81
rice: Mexican rice-stuffed
   peppers 125
   miso-glazed fish with sticky
      rice & greens 118
ricotta: gnocchi with mushrooms,
   spinach, ricotta, walnuts &
   lemon 134
Ritz crackers: Brie & chorizo
   savoury s'mores 62
rocket salad, caramelized onion
   & goat's cheese tarts with 64

salads: the best ever burrata
   salad 38
   lemon mayo slaw 56
   rocket salad 64
satay: peanut satay veg bao
   buns 138
sausages: pigs in blankets, Brie
   & cranberry sausage rolls 75
   sausage meatball pasta bake 93
   Scotch eggs 42
schnitzels, chicken Parmesan 98
scones, easy-peasy cheese &
   chive 59
Scotch eggs 42
shakshuka with butter beans 23
shawarma pitta pockets,
   chicken 47
slaws 56, 102
s'mores: Brie & chorizo savoury
   s'mores 62
   super-easy s'mores 171
soup, roasted tomato, bacon
   & basil 53
spanakopita bites 66
spinach: gnocchi with mushrooms,
   spinach, ricotta, walnuts &
   lemon 134
   harissa poached eggs with
      spinach & peppers 33
   quick & easy egg cups 25

spanakopita bites 66
spinach, sun-dried tomato
   & goat's cheese frittata 34
sticky teriyaki salmon traybake 111
sticky toffee ginger pudding 183
sweet potatoes: baked sweet
   potato with goat's cheese &
   sun-dried tomatoes 132

tacos: breaded prawn tacos 108
   burger tacos 100
   easy egg taco boats 17
tandoori baby potatoes, crispy 142
tartare sauce 116
tarts, caramelized onion & goat's
   cheese 64
Tenderstem broccoli with sesame,
   honey & lime 162
teriyaki salmon traybake, sticky 111
Thai turkey burgers 102
toffee: sticky toffee ginger
   pudding 183
tomatoes: baked sweet potato
   with goat's cheese & sun-dried
   tomatoes 132
   Boursin & tomato pasta 128
   chicken, pesto, sun-dried tomato
      & Parmesan wrap 50
   crostini with roasted tomatoes
      & goat's cheese 78
   roasted tomato, bacon & basil
      soup 53
   smoky shakshuka 23
   spinach, sun-dried tomato
      & goat's cheese frittata 34
tortilla boats: easy egg taco
   boats 17
traybake, sticky teriyaki salmon 111
truffle Parmesan fries 144
turkey burgers, Thai 102

vegetables: peanut satay veg bao
   buns 138
   roasted veggies 147

walnuts: gnocchi with mushrooms,
   spinach, ricotta, walnuts &
   lemon 134
wraps: breaded prawn tacos 108
   burger tacos 100
   chicken, pesto, sun-dried tomato
      & Parmesan wrap 50
   salmon fish finger wraps 56

yoghurt: chicken shawarma pitta
   pockets 47
   harissa yoghurt 137
   lime yoghurt sauce 157
Yorkshire puddings 152

Acknowledgements

I'd like to thank my mum and dad for going on (and on) about their air fryer a few years ago and convincing me to get one. You were right – it really did change everything, and now I go on (and on) about it to everyone I know.

My husband, for being endlessly patient when I refuse to let him in the kitchen while I'm cooking and filming for 'that TikTok thing'. Mr T is always my biggest backer.

My friends and family, for always hyping me up, keeping me going, and convincing me that maybe I could actually write a book. And my work colleagues, for trying out a lot of random air fryer treats throughout the week.

The lovely team at HarperCollins, for sliding into my inbox and helping turn all of this into a real, printed thing (eeeeeeeek!). And my agent, Issy, for guiding me smoothly through the process – and for the odd boujee cocktail to 'discuss the book' (wink wink, nudge nudge).

The 1 million-plus people who follow me on social – this is mostly down to you. Every like, comment, and share has got me here, so thank you from the bottom of my (slightly air fryer-shaped) heart.

Davina McCall, for that early podcast shout-out – a surreal moment that made everything start to feel real.

And finally, Oasis – for getting me through the writing process with your 2025 set list on repeat. Little by Little, I got through it!